CHILDREN'S EMPOWERMENT IN PLAY

Children's Empowerment in Play is an accessible insight into the vital place of play in children's development. The book focuses on three main themes of participation, voice and ownership, and explores ways to positively and naturally develop play in early years settings.

Drawing on primary research and presenting in-depth case studies of children in a range of play scenarios, Canning offers a framework for understanding play and its relationship with children's empowerment, and highlights play patterns and the ways in which practitioners can identify these. Chapters also cover:

- The research context for empowerment in play.
- The significance of play and empowerment in the lives of children.
- The power play can have, and indicators of empowering behaviour.
- Observing empowerment in play and the challenges of celebrating it.

Written for all those working with young children and students on early childhood courses, this book will transform how you understand and engage with children's experiences and learning

Natalie Canning is a Senior Lecturer in Early Childhood Education at The Open University, UK. Her background is in playwork and social work, supporting children to explore personal, social and emotional issues through play.

RESEARCH INFORMED PROFESSIONAL DEVELOPMENT FOR THE EARLY YEARS
TACTYC (Association for Professional Development in Early Years)

The books in this series each focus on a different aspect of research in early childhood which has direct implications for practice and policy. They consider the main research findings which should influence practitioner thinking and reflection and help them to question their own practice alongside activities to deepen knowledge and extend understanding of the issues. Readers will benefit from clear analysis, critique and interpretation of the key factors surrounding the research as well as exemplifications and case studies to illustrate the research-practice or research-policy links. Supporting the development of critical reflection and up to date knowledge, the books will be a core resource for all those educating and training early years practitioners.

Exploring the Contexts for Early Learning
Challenging the School Readiness Agenda
Rory McDowall Clark

Building Knowledge in Early Childhood Education
Young Children are Researchers
Jane Murray

Early Childhood Education and Care for Sustainability
International Perspectives
Valerie Huggins and David Evans

Places for Two-Year-Olds in the Early Years
Supporting Learning and Development
Jan Georgeson and Verity Campbell-Barr

Racialisation in Early Years Education
Black Children's Stories from the Classroom
Gina Houston

Children's Empowerment in Play
Participation, Voice and Ownership
Natalie Canning

CHILDREN'S EMPOWERMENT IN PLAY

Participation, Voice and Ownership

Natalie Canning

LONDON AND NEW YORK

First published 2020
by Routledge
2 Park Square, Milton Park, Abingdon, Oxon OX14 4RN

and by Routledge
52 Vanderbilt Avenue, New York, NY 10017

Routledge is an imprint of the Taylor & Francis Group, an informa business

© 2020 Natalie Canning

The right of Natalie Canning to be identified as author of this work has been asserted by her in accordance with sections 77 and 78 of the Copyright, Designs and Patents Act 1988.

All rights reserved. No part of this book may be reprinted or reproduced or utilised in any form or by any electronic, mechanical, or other means, now known or hereafter invented, including photocopying and recording, or in any information storage or retrieval system, without permission in writing from the publishers.

Trademark notice: Product or corporate names may be trademarks or registered trademarks, and are used only for identification and explanation without intent to infringe.

First edition published 2020

British Library Cataloguing in Publication Data
A catalogue record for this book is available from the British Library

Library of Congress Cataloging-in-Publication Data
Names: Canning, Natalie, author.
Title: Children's empowerment in play : participation, voice and ownership / Natalie Canning.
Description: Abingdon, Oxon ; New York, NY : Routledge, 2020. | Series: Tactyc | Includes bibliographical references and index.
Identifiers: LCCN 2019043706 (print) | LCCN 2019043707 (ebook) | ISBN 9781138322288 (hardback) | ISBN 9781138322295 (paperback) | ISBN 9780429452178 (ebook)
Subjects: LCSH: Play. | Childhood development. | Early childhood education.
Classification: LCC LB1139.35.P55 C36 2020 (print) | LCC LB1139.35.P55 (ebook) | DDC 372.21--dc23
LC record available at https://lccn.loc.gov/2019043706
LC ebook record available at https://lccn.loc.gov/2019043707

ISBN: 978-1-138-32228-8 (hbk)
ISBN: 978-1-138-32229-5 (pbk)
ISBN: 978-0-429-45217-8 (ebk)

Typeset in Bembo
by Taylor & Francis Books

With thanks to Liz Caulfield for kindly providing the illustrations for this book.

CONTENTS

List of illustrations   *viii*
Foreword   *x*

Introduction   1

1 The context of researching children's empowerment in play   6

2 The significance of play and empowerment in young children's lives   18

3 The power of play   29

4 Indicators of empowering play behaviour   44

5 Exploring children's participation, voice and ownership through play   62

6 Observing empowerment in play   75

7 The challenges of celebrating empowerment in play   90

Conclusion   102

References   *104*
Index   *112*

ILLUSTRATIONS

Figures

1.1 Visual map of research settings and case study children	7
1.2 A multimodal research approach	13
1.3 Selection of case study children's choices of their favourite play	16
2.1 Amy creating her dragon	25
3.1 Playing with dripping water	33
4.1 Milo and his friend comparing lengths	45
4.2 Lucy standing on a crate at the rural private day nursery	49
4.3 Jade and friends rolling the pipe	52
4.4 Milo demonstrating his show-jumping skills	55
4.5 Michael and Tom with the toy cars	58
4.6 The empowerment framework: video data codes (in italics) and their relationship to the super-themes (in bold) and sub-themes (underlined) of the research	61
5.1 Edward taking the lead in den making	64
5.2 Harry playing dead	69
5.3 Michael making a leap for the pole	73
6.1 The empowerment framework	76
6.2 Empowerment framework with prompt questions to guide educator observations	76
6.3 The moment the stick breaks in two	79
6.4 Small world play	82
6.5 The boys at the water butt	85
7.1 The empowerment framework	91

Tables

2.1	Description and time codes of Amy's play	26
3.1	Description and time codes of Harry's play	34
4.1	Coding Milo's play	47
4.2	Coding Lucy and Emma's play	50
4.3	Coding of Jade's rolling the pipe play	53
4.4	Coding Milo's imaginative play	56
4.5	Coding Michael's problem-solving play	59
5.1	Coding participation	65
5.2	Coding voice	68
5.3	Coding ownership	72
6.1	Empowerment framework prompt questions in a grid	78

FOREWORD

*Professor Emerita Janet Moyles and
Professor Jane Payler*

Welcome to the sixth volume in the new, inspiring TACTYC book series. As part of the Association for Professional Development in the Early Years, TACTYC members believe that effective early years policies and practices should be informed by an understanding of the findings and implications of high quality, robust research. TACTYC focuses on developing the knowledge base of all those concerned with early years education and care by creating, reviewing and disseminating research findings and by encouraging critical and constructive discussion to foster reflective attitudes in practitioners. Such a need has been evident in the resounding success of events such as our Conferences where speakers make clear connections between research and practice for delegates. Early years practitioners and those who support their professional development engage enthusiastically with early childhood research and understand how it is likely to impact upon, and enhance, practice. They acknowledge that research has a distinct role to play in effective work in early years education and care, and that they should be part of a 'research-rich education system'.

TACTYC is an organisation with a specific focus on the professional development of all those involved in early childhood with the express purpose of improving practices to enhance the well-being of young children. Its reputation for quality research and writing includes its international *Early Years* journal. This book series is popular with those who value the journal as it will add to its range and scope. Our aim for the series is to help those who educate and train early years practitioners at all levels to understand the implications and practical interpretation of recent research, and to offer a rationale for improving the quality and reach of practice in early years education and care

It is not always easy for busy trainers and practitioners to access contemporary research and translate it into informed and reflective practice. These books promote the benefits of applying research in an informed way to develop quality pedagogical practices. Each individual book in this series explores a range of different topics within a theme. This book considers the issues involved in *providing children with empowering opportunities for play*. Natalie's book teases out the implications of research and theory and presents these in a clear, unambiguous way, while acknowledging the often-complex relationships between what we know and what is possible in practice.

Natalie explains that, at the core of her book, is 'analysis of play experiences of seven children, how they react and interact with their peers and how their experiences support processes of empowerment'. In analysing children's experiences using video case studies and how they interact with peers, the issue of children's empowerment becomes paramount. The book examines adult participants' interpretations of children's play and shows how, despite avowed intentions to support children's interests and individual needs, much of practice centred on adult input and structure with very limited opportunities for children to develop their own play interests.

Natalie's three main questions are:

- In what ways can child-initiated, social play empower children?
- What is a valid and useful definition of children's empowerment in play?
- How can articulating the significance of children's empowerment in play support early childhood practice?

The book argues that early childhood professionals need to provide more opportunities for 'uninterrupted child-initiated, social play to support empowering experiences'. Using examples of children's play and exploring these from the perspective of empowerment can initiate such developments in professional practice. The book therefore contributes significantly to our understanding of this important aspect of the early years field and reflects continuing interest in play and children's empowerment.

The claim is frequently made that policies are 'evidence-based' but this is not the same as rigorous, impartial research such as that in this book. Many policy and practice documents purport to be based on 'evidence', but this depends to a large extent on the political framework and ideology in place at different periods in time – few governments have the scope in their relatively short elected periods to give strategic consideration to the complex implications of different research outcomes for policies and practice. What is politically and economically expedient at the time is too often the driving force behind decisions about young children and their families.

All the writers in this series have been asked to present their particular focus, and to outline the issues and challenges within that framework relevant for early years practitioners. Exploring aspects of early years practice, based on research and sound theoretical underpinning, the writers will offer guidance on how findings can be analysed and interpreted to inform the continuing process of developing high quality early years practice. They will examine the research background to each topic and offer considered views on why the situation is as it is, and how it might move forward within the frameworks of imposed curricula and assessments. They will offer thoughtful advice to practitioners for dealing with the challenges faced within that particular focus and will suggest relevant follow-up reading and web-based materials to support further reflection, practice and curriculum implementation. Each book will also identify where further research is needed and will help tutors, trainers and practitioners to understand how they can contribute to research in this field.

Early years education and care is universally contentious, especially in relation to how far those outside the field, e.g. politicians and policy-makers, should intervene in deciding what constitutes successful early years pedagogy, curriculum and assessment. The main focus of the series is on practice, policy and provision in UK, but writers will also draw on international research perspectives, as there is a great deal to learn from colleagues in other national contexts.

The series particularly targets readers qualified at Level 6, or students on such courses, preparing for roles in which they will be expected to educate and train other practitioners in effective early years practices. There will be many others who will find the books invaluable: leaders of early years settings, who often have an education, training and professional development role in relation to their staff (and may well be qualified at Level 6 or beyond) will similarly find the series useful in their work. Academics and new researchers who support the training and development of graduate leaders in early years will also appreciate the books in this series. Readers will benefit from clear analysis, critique and interpretation of the key factors surrounding the research as well as exemplifications and case studies to illustrate the links between research and policy as well as research and practice. The books will support the development of critical reflection and up-to-date knowledge, and will be a core resource for all those educating and training early years practitioners.

In summary, research-based early years practice is a relatively new field as much of practitioners' work with young children over recent years has been based on the implementation of policy documents, which are often not grounded in rigorous, clear, unambiguous research evidence. The main aim of the TACTYC series is to help tutors and trainers to enable practitioners to become more informed advocates for provision of high quality services for children and their families. This will be achieved by promoting the benefits of applying research in an informed way to develop the quality of practice, in this instance, regarding children's play, empowerment and the role of adults.

INTRODUCTION

The study of children and what is important for their emotional well-being in early childhood has at its centre an ongoing debate about the best ways in which to support children's personal, social and emotional development (Layard et al., 2014). The changing political agendas over the last decade along with shifts in practice fuelled by different national and regional funding opportunities in the UK have resulted in a patchwork of research into diverse and wide-ranging areas of childhood (Waller, 2014). This book keeps in focus two established perspectives about childhood: first that children are socialised according to the expectations and patterns of a particular culture at a particular time (Mayall, 2002), and second that children are 'active subjects, not objects' in their worlds (Alldred, 2000, p. 150). Towards the end of the last decade increasing concern was being expressed that children were experiencing unprecedented levels of intervention into their lives, from academic expectations, surveillance and restrictions on their mobility, suggesting that childhood was becoming an 'era marked by both a sustained assault on children and a concern for children' (James et al., 1998, p. 3).

Why play?

Changing social patterns have contributed to the debate surrounding the significance of children's play (Moyles, 2010; Hughes, 2001; Lester and Russell, 2008). That play is a key component in children's cognitive and social development is now recognised by policy advisors and increased investment has been made at local, regional and national level into providing children's play opportunities both in early childhood settings and in local communities (Wood, 2010). There are now significant data about children's lives, taking into consideration their perspectives and listening to children's views, which reflect some of the developments of wider attitudes towards children as social participants (MacNaughton, 2005). The core of this book is the analysis of play experiences of seven children, how they react and interact with their peers and how their experiences support processes of empowerment, along with analysis of adult participants' interpretations. These analyses are then used to critically reflect on the broader current issues around the significance of play.

In discussions with early childhood educators about their settings and how they implement a play-based curriculum it is evident that they are enthusiastic about supporting children's development through play and consider their settings to be centred on following children's interests and meeting their individual needs. In order to evaluate practice, settings were visited to observe how they supported and implemented a play-based curriculum. A range of practices was observed, mainly focused on children achieving outcome-based activities, with adult input, structure and guidance. Play was interpreted in different ways, but there was very little child-initiated play where children were able to choose what they wanted to do, have access to the resources they wanted to play with or have the time that would be needed to follow their own interests.

The analysis of observations in settings and adults' interpretations of children's play evidence not only the diversity of understandings of the term 'play', but also indicates how children can be empowered or dis-empowered by decisions made, actions taken and reactions to children in practice. Discussion with educators shows that they consider play to be significant for children's development and genuinely believe they are providing a play-based curriculum. However, they had not considered how their interaction with children impacted on children's play or children's capacity to be empowered by play. The notion of empowerment is generally something acknowledged as important, but educators through discussion were unable to articulate what it meant or looked like in practice.

A review of previous research into empowerment in early childhood found that there is limited literature on the topic and that most relates to the empowerment of early childhood educators rather than children (Howard, 2010; McInnes et al., 2011; Moyles, 2010; Pramling Samuelsson and Carlsson, 2008; Rogers, 2011). In the wealth of literature relating to children's play more generally, terminology such as 'confidence', 'choice' and 'agency' are associated with play, but no links are made with empowerment and this suggested a gap in research specifically about children's empowerment in play. One of the aims of the research presented in this book is to develop understandings surrounding early childhood practice in order to develop a case for children being given greater opportunities for uninterrupted child-initiated, social play to support empowering experiences. Through considering children's empowerment, this book provides supporting arguments for early childhood professionals that will support prioritising particular approaches to play in practice and thus place greater value on the process of empowerment.

Throughout the book three main questions are posed:

In what ways can child-initiated, social play empower children?

There are many definitions and positions on play and so, by focusing upon child-initiated, social play, a specific perspective on child–child relationships in play is adopted throughout the book. This places children at the centre of the play process, considering the choices and decisions they make and the ways in which those choices contribute to their play experiences. The question explores not only a view of play, but also the interactions between children, how they participate and contribute in play situations, how they use the environment and resources around them, and how early childhood professionals respond and react when children are in charge of their own play. The play environments that children encounter are also to some extent constructed opportunities for children's play, organised by an adult. How these spaces mediate opportunities for empowerment are also considered.

What is a valid and useful definition of children's empowerment in play?

The focus on child-initiated, social play provides a basis from which to critically examine the concept of empowerment and its significance in children's play. Developing a definition of empowerment as the basis for observations of children's play is necessary to support a deeper understanding of the processes involved in children's empowerment in play and how empowerment is made more visible in practice.

How can articulating the significance of children's empowerment in play support early childhood practice?

The examples of play throughout the chapters in this book consider what children do when they engage in child-initiated, social play. They illustrate how looking at what happens in children's play from a perspective of a process of empowerment can initiate developments in professional practice. There are examples of different approaches to observing and recording children's interactions through their participation, ownership of play situations and how they express themselves through play.

An approach to researching play

Investigations into children's play have spanned diverse theoretical and disciplinary landscapes encompassing qualitative and quantitative studies, from experimental to interpretative paradigms. Research has reflected different schools of thought, focus and agendas within different disciplines such as sociology, psychology, philosophy and anthropology (Silverman, 2001; Mason, 2002). The study of children, James et al. (1998) argue, requires interdisciplinary investigation and this book draws on insights from various social science disciplines. At the centre of the research carried out for this book are children's experiences of play and the question of how play can support a process of empowerment. These are explored through the collection of video data of case study children in different play contexts. The research is also supported by interviews with parents and early childhood educators to explore their views about children's empowerment and its significance in everyday practice.

Seven children participated in the research located within a 30-mile radius of each other in central England. The children attended a range of early childhood contexts and they had a range of family situations, home environments and socio-economic backgrounds. There is significant variation in social and cultural views of children's play, but it was necessary to restrict the sample size and location of the study which meant predominantly white British families were representative of the communities in which the research took place.

The structure of the book

The first chapter introduces the children that took part in the research and who feature in the examples throughout the chapters. The settings they attended are described and the way in which some children attended multiple settings is explained. Children's play was observed in their day-care provision, but also at home with their siblings and friends. This gave a clearer picture of the children's interests and preferences. It also enabled an understanding of how their play was consistent or changed when the environment altered.

Chapters 2 and 3 outline the existing literature in relation to play and power. Chapter 2 explores the significance of play in young children's lives and the multi-faceted views of empowerment from different disciplines. Children's right to play and the complexities of defining play and exploring play discourses are examined. Power relationships between children and adults are examined in Chapter 3 and in particular questions who holds power in play situations? This underpins the discussion about power and truth and how these two concepts impact on children's play experiences. The role of the early childhood educator is analysed in relation to changing attitudes towards pedagogy and working within a curriculum. The chapter concludes with a definition of empowerment which supports further discussion and analysis in later chapters.

Chapter 4 considers the indicators of empowerment that can be recognised in children's play under three broad areas of: children's choices and their decisions; the context of children's play; and the interactions between children. The chapter identifies five sub-themes – Motivation, Coordination, Imagination, Problem Solving and Empathy – that differentiate the layered picture of knowledge and understanding about children's empowerment. Examples illustrating each of the sub-themes taken from the video and interview data and perspectives of parents and educators are also included in this chapter. At the end of this chapter the empowerment framework is introduced.

Chapter 5 explores the three super-themes that became apparent as significant for children to be empowered in play. These are the need to feel part of the play in some way, to be able to participate. The ability to voice opinions and to be acknowledged as part of the play process is also essential and the feeling that they have ownership over what is happening in the play. The three super-themes of participation, voice and ownership are illustrated with examples from the case study children's play in a range of contexts and form the core of the empowerment framework.

Chapter 6 demonstrates how the empowerment framework can be used as a tool for observing play. It focuses upon children's actions and interactions and how they can be interpreted in relation to empowerment. Examples illustrate the process of empowerment and how the framework works in practice. Reflections from educators in using the framework are significant in enabling a shift in focus from competence-based observation to empowering experience observations.

Finally, Chapter 7 discusses the challenges of play and empowerment and revisits the broad questions outlined in the introduction. Key aspects of this chapter include how children's play environments support processes of empowerment and the influence of culture on children's choices and decisions in play. Values and beliefs about play and empowerment are revisited and their impact on practice evaluated.

Throughout, the book argues that adults' focus on children's play should centre on transformative experiences where the unpredictability and open-endedness of play is celebrated. The process of empowerment in play is not determined by the context, but is influenced by children's actions and reactions within that context. Empowerment therefore is not restricted by the environment or resources within it, but can be accessed by children through their interactions and the possibilities available to them through play.

1
THE CONTEXT OF RESEARCHING CHILDREN'S EMPOWERMENT IN PLAY

In this chapter the case study children that feature throughout the book are introduced, providing an insight into their daily routines and play preferences. The early childhood settings are described and the cross-over between the children and the different settings they attended explained.

The early childhood settings and case study children are based in one geographic location, in central England. It was important, given a sociocultural approach, that a range of early childhood contexts, offering different play experiences to children, were represented (Brooker, 2002; Rogoff, 2003). The range of settings included different types of ownership, for example, private, for-profit settings and a local authority resourced children's centre. This had a potential impact on how the settings were managed and their philosophy towards children's play (Brooker, 2011). There were four early childhood settings in total, two within a city centre – a children's centre and private day nursery, and two in more rural locations – a childminder and private day nursery. The demographic of the city is a largely white population, with a range of socio-economic backgrounds and the case study children and families reflected these characteristics.

From the children attending these settings, seven children were selected as the focus for case studies. This selection was based on the children's age; an even mix between girls and boys; family situations, for example proximity of extended family, siblings and nuclear family arrangements; regular attendance at the selected settings; and willingness of parents to be involved in the research. The seven case study children were identified in liaison with the participating settings and their parents. Three of the children attended more than one setting and this provided insight into their play at different locations and with different children.

Figure 1.1 is a visual representation of the settings and where each of the children attended.

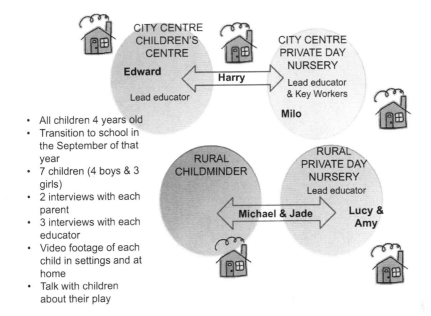

FIGURE 1.1 Visual map of research settings and case study children

Age of the children

The sample was a mixture of four boys and three girls. They had attended their respective settings for at least 12 months and were all four years old. Four-year-old children were purposely chosen as they were able to express themselves and engage in more detailed, imaginative play and social interaction. They were all preparing to start school in the September of that year and were able to express their opinion in play through different modes of communication, both verbal and non-verbal, and use their imagination in play with each other. Fromberg and Bergen (2015) suggest that four-year-old children are at an interesting juncture in their lives as they are about to leave the familiarity of their early childhood setting, where they have formed strong relationships with staff and other children and are confident and self-assured in the routines and expectations of their surroundings. The children were aware of the impending transition to more formal learning in UK primary schools through 'taster' sessions at their new school, meeting their new teacher and classmates. They were all aware of the imminent changes and to some extent this was reflected in their play.

The settings

City centre private day nursery

The setting is a for-profit small business with 89 places. Organised over two levels, the pre-school room, with a mixture of three-and-a-half- and four-year-old children, is located on the first floor. There is access to an enclosed garden area, which is concrete paved with placed resources such as tractor tyres, climbing frame equipment and children's bicycles. The pre-school room is resourced with age appropriate toys and open-ended resources and children have the opportunity for child-led play and structured adult-led activities within the daily routine of the setting.

Visits to the city centre private day nursery coincided with the case study children's attendance and mainly took place after lunch until home time. Once lunch had been cleared children had child-initiated play time for approximately an hour and a half. If the weather was good, then the children would have the opportunity to go outside, but this involved going down a set of stairs and along a corridor to the outside space and had to fit in with other age group rooms as there was not enough space for two groups of children to be outside at once. During the inside play time, children could access any of the resources, but sometimes had to negotiate for space on tables and also take turns on the computer and indoor climbing frame structures. Towards the end of the afternoon, children were encouraged to tidy up and then have a snack, after which there was a story and then songs would be sung in anticipation for collection by parents and carers. A typical timetable of the children's afternoon activity involved:

1pm	Lunch
2pm	Child-initiated play either inside or outside or a combination of both. If outside or a combination at least 15 minutes spent getting to and from the outside space (1.5 hours)
3.30pm	Tidy up time where children are encouraged to put all the resources away
3.45pm	Snack time (including handwashing and toileting)
4.10pm	Story time
4.30pm	Home time

Two children, Milo and Harry, were the focus in this setting. Harry also attended the children's centre.

City centre children's centre

The setting is a local authority owned children's centre which is open access to the local community. The centre provides a range of services for families with children under the age of five years and the focus of the study concentrated on the 'stay and play' sessions which were organised in the forest school. The 'stay and play' sessions required a parent to have overall responsibility for their children and therefore only one qualified professional was required. A number of different children and their parents came each week to the outside space which consisted of a small woodland area. The educator had a theme each time, spending the first ten minutes around a central 'camp' area and then allowing the rest of the two-hour session for child-initiated play. Parents mainly stayed around the 'camp' area for the duration of the session whilst the children played around them.

The visits to the children's centre mainly took place in the morning. Parents and children would meet in the café and then make their way as a group to the forest school. The first ten minutes of the session were led by the early childhood professional who welcomed children and parents and introduced a theme such as the story of the 'Gruffalo' (*The Gruffalo* is a children's book about a mouse who takes a walk in the woods and comes across a bear-like creature called the Gruffalo). Children were then free to explore and play in the woodland for the remaining two hours. They did not have to follow the theme introduced by the educator, but there were resources available which supported the theme which were kept in the central 'camp' area for that session. The early childhood educator was on hand to talk to parents and engaged with the children as and when they asked for help. At the end of the session children and parents shared lunch in the café. A typical timetable of the children's morning activities involved:

10am	Parents and children meet in the café
10.15am	Everyone walks together to the woodland area and meets in the camp area
10.20am	Lead educator introduces the sessions focus
10.30am	Child-initiated play in the woodland area (two hours)
12.30pm	Session ends and parents and children have lunch together in the café

Two children, Edward and Harry, were the focus in this setting. Harry also attended the city centre private day nursery.

Rural private day nursery

The nursery is a for-profit small business with 52 places. Based within an old village primary school the setting is on one level and children in the pre-school room are a mix of three- and four-year-olds. There are two outdoor areas, a large field with a constructed canopy for shelter and large outdoor adventure equipment comprising of a wooden bridge, platform and slide pole and a more conventional steel slide built into a bank. The other area is a more structured playground with a tarmac area for bicycles and a grass area where large tractor tyres have been stood on end and sunk into the ground, providing a climbing structure. The pre-school room is resourced with a variety of toys and materials for activities such as painting and model making and children have the opportunity for sustained child-initiated play outside, woven around indoor adult-directed activities in the daily routine.

The visits to the rural private day nursery mainly took place in the morning until lunchtime. Children had an hour of play where staff laid out resources for the children. There was some flexibility, in that if a child wanted to play with something else, they were allowed, but had to put away the item they had finished with first. A formal snack time followed and then outside play for an hour, regardless of the weather and usually in the field. The outside play was totally child-initiated and the large space encouraged physical play. Lunch was served when all of the children were back inside. A typical timetable of the children's morning activity involved:

9am	Child initiated play – as and when children arrive they join in play or choose their own resources to play with (one hour)
10am	Snack time (including handwashing and toileting)
11am	Outside child-initiated play either in the field or playground (one hour). At least ten minutes spent on organising footwear and coats
12pm	Preparing for lunch (handwashing, toileting, setting tables)
12.30pm	Lunch

Four children, Amy, Lucy, Jade and Michael, were the focus. Jade and Michael also attended the childminder setting.

Childminder

The setting is based in a home location and registered with the local authority for up to six children under the age of eight. Children have access to three downstairs play rooms and an open plan kitchen area. Outside has a tarmac drive and large flat grass area and, inside, the home has a variety of toys and open-ended materials that children could play with. There is easy access between the house and garden and children were free to move between the two areas as they wished. The routine was unstructured and child-initiated, with assistance from an adult only being given when requested by a child.

The visits to the childminder took place in the afternoon. Children had been provided with lunch before coming to the setting and so could access resources to play with straight away. The afternoon was unstructured with the childminder checking that the children were safe and answering any questions they had. The childminder was mainly located in the kitchen where she could see both the garden and play rooms if different children were in different spaces and snacks and drinks were provided as and when children requested them. There was a mix of ages at the childminder setting; the older children supported the younger ones who wanted to be involved in the same things such as making a necklace with beads. Play continued until parents arrived and collected their children. There was a length of time where parents chatted to the childminder and had coffee and snacks before leaving the setting. A typical timetable of the children's afternoon activities involved:

1pm	Children arrive and offered a drink and some discussion of what they want to play with
1.15pm	Children access resources and child-initiated play (two hours)
3.15pm	Children offered a snack and drink
3.30pm	Parents start arriving to pick up children

Two children, the twins, Jade and Michael, were the focus in the setting. They also attended the rural private day nursery.

Case study children

Edward

Edward lives on the outskirts of the city with his mother and father and new-born baby sister. He has extended family close by and the family has a dog. Edward attends the children's centre twice a week and is looked after at home the rest of the time. Edward looks older than his four years and is the tallest child at the children's centre.

Harry

Harry lives in the city centre with his mother and father. He is 'a long awaited' only child (as described by his mother). The family is not originally from the area and there are no extended family members close by. Harry attends the children's centre twice a week and the city centre private day nursery for two days per week.

Milo

Milo lives in the city centre with his mother and father. He has a younger sister and extended family members close by. He attends the private day nursery three days per week and is at home for the remainder of the time.

Michael and Jade

Michael and Jade are twins. They live outside of the city in a rural hamlet with their mother and father. Their father works away from home for sustained periods of time. They have extended family approximately an hour's drive away and visit them some weekends and holidays. Michael and Jade have an older sister and a grown up half brother and sister who do not live with them, but are visited on a regular basis. Michael and Jade attend the rural private day nursery five mornings per week and a childminder five afternoons per week.

Lucy

Lucy lives outside of the city centre in a rural village with her mother and father. Her father is in the military and works away from home for sustained periods of time. She has a younger sister and extended family who she visits on a regular basis. She attends the rural private day nursery five days per week.

Amy

Amy lives outside of the city in a rural village with her mother. She is an only child with no extended family members close by and limited contact with her father. She attends the rural private day nursery five days per week and has done so since she was six months old.

A multimodal approach to researching children's empowerment in play

Case studies offer ways to construct understanding and learning from information gathered from multiple sources (Simons, 1996; Yin, 2012). By finding out more about particular children's lives through a multimodal approach (Dicks et al., 2011), interviewing parents and practitioners, by observing children in different contexts and by engaging children to think about their experiences through talking to them, commonalities were established between the various cases. This allowed a more comprehensive understanding of children's empowerment in play. Studying play from more than one standpoint supported a detailed exploration of the process of empowerment and permitted coordination of the data to 'map out, or explain more fully, the richness and complexity of human behaviour' (Cohen et al., 2007, p. 254). Figure 1.2 shows the different ways data was gathered to form a multimodal approach.

The multimodal approach provided a framework for analysis (Kress, 2009) and the development of case studies allowed for multiple viewpoints from parents, practitioners and the children themselves on how they experienced social play. Central to all of this was the relationships between the researcher and participants as well as triangulation of the data and multimodal nature of analysis supporting the validation of the study (Dicks et al., 2011; Flewitt, 2006).

Non-participant observations: video recordings

The aim of the research was to explore child-initiated play without adult interaction. Video recordings captured all of the play that the case study children were involved in during each visit and the multiple visits to different settings ensured that a variety of play was captured. In the cases of three of the children, Jade, Michael and Harry, play was filmed in more than one early childhood setting because they attended multiple settings. The video data were collected with a hand-held digital video camera which had a built-in timer visible on the side opening monitor. This allowed discreet filming to minimise children's awareness of the camera and for the camera to move with the children as they played. The camera also allowed still photographs from the video footage to be printed which formed the central part of talking with the children after the observations had been completed.

In each filming opportunity the camera was positioned a comfortable distance from the case study children and the zoom features of the camera helped minimise the impact of filming children's play. This was especially useful outside where children had

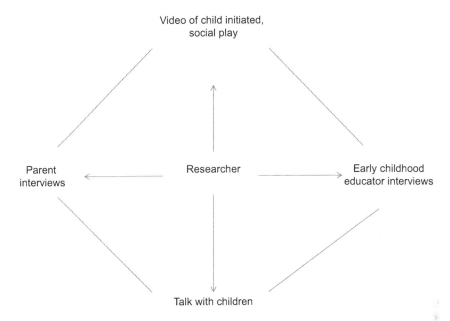

FIGURE 1.2 A multimodal research approach

access to a large space in three of the settings. The footage was concerned with the interactions of the children, rather than what they said, and so the camera could be positioned at a distance to minimise any self-conscious play behaviour. It was important that the video was as non-intrusive as possible and that children were not distracted by the camera or filming. Adult influence in the children's play would have changed the dynamics; however, O'Reilly (2009) argues that all observations involve some participation and even acting 'as if not there' influences the situation being observed. She considers that non-participant observation is more about limited interaction. The presence of the video camera to some extent had an effect on the children and staff, and perhaps made the children more self-aware in their play because in the first few minutes when the video was recording some children would ask why the video camera was there. Children were reminded of the orientation visit when they were able to look at the camera and ask questions about the research. Once an explanation had been given, children seemed satisfied to continue with their play. Over the visits to the different settings, children were less inquisitive and appeared to ignore the camera to a large extent.

Time sampling

Initial video recordings continuously filmed children's play, but this resulted in lengthy sequences of film that were difficult to organise and analyse. Using time sampling provided a focus and parameters for the observations. The children were making decisions about what, who and where they played within the boundaries of a setting and the time sample provided an element of structure and organisation in gathering visual data.

The observations with the video camera were captured in approximately two-minute time samples which are considered the optimum time for this type of observation (Wright, 1960). The two-minute time frame was appropriate as much of the children's play in all of the settings and home contexts seemed to arrive at a natural pause at this point, before the play developed further, came to a conclusion or turned into something else. If children's play continued beyond two minutes, the camera would be stopped and re-started immediately, providing a marker point. The camera recorded the majority of the case study children's child-initiated social play in the observation sessions that were agreed with the educators and parents.

Organisation of observations

Visits to the settings for filming were arranged to cover the expected attendance of the case study children and most of them had a regular attendance routine. Consequently, visits to focus on individual children were made on the same day of the week, same session, week on week over a four-week period. Each of the settings followed their own weekly routines and the filming fitted into the settings structure of activities. Each session in the different settings lasted approximately 2.5 hours and consisted of either a morning or afternoon visit where video footage was captured when the case study children were engaged in child-initiated, social play. The actual play situations could not be planned and it meant that there could be no expectation about the amount of data that might be collected on each visit, or the type and situation of play that children would engage with. For example, it was the setting's decision if play was inside or outside, for how long and the type of resources available to children.

Filming in the home of each of the seven case study children was arranged at the convenience of the parent and only one visit to the home environment to film was made for each of the case study children. In the home environment the video footage collected for each child was between 10 and 15 minutes and it was the child's choice of where and what to play with, sometimes in negotiation with the parent.

Early childhood educator and parent interviews

Interviews were conducted with early childhood educators and parents of the case study children to explore views, knowledge and understanding about children's empowerment and its significance in contributing to children's social and emotional development. The interviews were organised at different stages of the study so that views from educators and parents about empowerment could be established at the beginning of the research and could be reflected upon at the end, supported with video stimulated review from the video footage of children's play (Forman, 1999).

All of the interviews were semi-structured, asking questions specific to issues of empowerment, but tailored to the context of the interviewee's setting or child. There can be unequal power relationships between interviewer and interviewee if the interviewer is perceived to have all the answers and therefore authority in an interview situation (Mishler, 1986). Consequently, interviewees may try to tailor their answers to what they think the interviewer wants to hear rather than being confident to express their own opinion. The interviews attempted to put the participant at ease and ask questions directly relating to their knowledge about the focused case study child. Through seeking opinion rather than answering questions the power dynamics between interviewer and interviewee were more balanced.

In the city centre private day nursery a number of different early childhood educators were involved in the interviews as the case study children had different key workers. The room leader participated in the first interview, whilst the key workers for the two children participated in separate second interviews. For the third interview, the key workers and room leader participated in separate interviews to review the video footage. These interviews allowed the collection of different views with different levels of experience and knowledge of the case study children. In the childminder, rural private day nursery and city centre children's centre, those interviewed were the same for all of the interviews.

The first two sets of interviews lasted between 30 and 45 minutes depending on the responses to the questions. In their first interview some educators were able to link their understanding of empowerment to knowledge gained from studying for a degree, and in the second interview all were able to talk at length about the personalities and play preferences of the case study children. The third interviews lasted longer, between one and 1.5 hours as the practitioners reviewed between four and five video sequences of their case study child and were asked to comment on each one in relation to semi-structured questions based on the play behaviour of the child and how that may link to a process of empowerment.

Parent interviews

The interviews with the seven parents of case study children took place in their home environments and were all conducted with the mothers of the case study children. The interviews ranged from 15 to 30 minutes in length depending on their responses. Some were more confident than others in engaging in a dialogue about the idea of empowerment, but all were able to give insights into their values and beliefs about bringing up their children, what they thought their child gained from playing with others and the differences between their child's social and solitary play and how that impacted on the choices they made for their child's social engagements and education. The second interview, where mothers reviewed the video footage, gave them insight into their child's activities in a different context and they were able to talk about comparisons between their child's preferences and behaviour.

Throughout the research process a handwritten reflective account was kept, detailing thoughts and observations about how children made their choices and decisions in the different play situations they encountered, how other children responded to those choices and notes on the different interactions children had with educators throughout the visit. For each entry, the date and location were

	**Amy** sitting on one of the tractor tyres singing with Jade and Lucy outside at the rural private day nursery. Amy's response: 'I'm laughing'
	**Lucy** at home in her bedroom, dressing up with her pet dog in the background and her sister just out of shot. Lucy's response: 'I like to pretend and play with pretty things'
	**Michael** climbing a pole in order to slide down it, outside at the rural private day nursery. Michael's response: 'I wanted to get to the top and I did it and it was fun and I beat Tom'
	**Harry** outside sitting around the camp fire at the Forest School in the city centre children's centre. Harry's response: 'It's raining, I'm wet and catching the rain. They're my friends, it's fun'

FIGURE 1.3 Selection of case study children's choices of their favourite play

noted. At one point in the research observations and interviews were taking place in three different settings, involving five of the children, so the diary helped to clarify thoughts and record specific details which may have influenced the children's play or practitioners' responses. The diary also assisted in formulating possible themes emerging from the collective play across settings and contexts.

Talking with children

Gaining children's views was an integral part of the research and at the end of the study, once all of the filming and interviews had taken place, the case study children were asked about their likes and dislikes about play. The discussion was supported by still photographs printed from the video footage which showed the case study child playing in different contexts and with different resources. These conversations with children were conducted at the end of the study to avoid children feeling self-conscious about their play or thinking about what they were doing and why when they were being filmed. Children were given smiley and sad face stickers to choose the play which they enjoyed the most and the least and then asked why they had chosen those particular photographs. The talks with children were conducted in the child's setting with an educator close by to support the child if needed or in their own home with a parent in close proximity, but not influencing the child. All of the children were happy to choose their favourite photograph and each gave a brief explanation of why they liked that photograph the best. Figure 1.3 details a selection of the children's responses about why they had chosen a particular picture to represent their favourite play.

The children were reluctant to put sad faces on the photographs and most of the photographs in fact had smiley faces on them. So an extra smiley face sticker was given and the children asked to choose their most favourite photograph of them playing. It is important that children are given the opportunity to have a say, that they are acknowledged in their opinions and engaged as far as possible in discussion (Matthews, 2003). The smiley faces were not intended primarily as a scale of 'liking', but were used as a way to get children talking about their play experiences. The extra smiley face was used to ask them specific questions about their favourite play and why they enjoyed that so much.

Summary

Detailing the context of the research and the practicalities of videoing, interviewing and talking to children gives an indication of how the play examples and quotes from educators and parents were collected and used for the basis of developing a definition of empowerment. The following chapters explore the nature of empowerment and the implications for children and early childhood practice.

2

THE SIGNIFICANCE OF PLAY AND EMPOWERMENT IN YOUNG CHILDREN'S LIVES

This chapter sets out why empowerment is important for children and why play is the best way to understand the processes involved in being empowered. Play is also a process, recognising children's own agendas and motivations and how they can contribute to empowering experiences. Understanding the power of play is based upon child-initiated, social play and contributes to the debate about how play supports children's personal, social and emotional development.

There are two main trains of thought that underpin early childhood practice in the UK (Stephen, 2010). One is that early childhood provision should be child-centred and follow the child's interests in relation to the choices they make, who they choose to engage with and how they participate in activities. Allowing children to 'wallow' in their play provides an insight into children's interests and preferences (Bruce, 1991). The other idea is that play can be formalised into a series of engaging activities which forefront learning opportunities and achievable outcomes. Wood (2010, p. 16) believes that this approach means that play is 'intrinsically bound with contemporary policies of education, because it is subject to regulation and management' based on the ideology of education at the time. Consequently play becomes tied to educational versions of learning ideas rather than an independent process that is personally directed and intrinsically motivated (Playwork Principles Scrutiny Group, 2005).

The term 'play' is used and interpreted in many ways in early childhood and this depends very much on local, historical and sociocultural contexts and traditions. As Sutton Smith (1997) points out, play is also interpreted according to research interests, as well as cultural influences or personal emphasis. Even the pioneers of play, such as Froebel (1782–1852), McMillan (1860–1931), Isaacs (1885–1948), Steiner (1861–1925) and Piaget (1896–1980), placed an emphasis on different elements of play depending on their research interests and experiences. The subjective nature of interpreting play adds to the complexity of attempting to work towards a definition of play. Consequently the unique characteristics and qualities that children express during play through what they choose to do, who they play with and how their play evolves in the moment and over time means that close observation of play, as the dominant way in which children express their preferences, is necessary to reach an understanding of play, especially in relation to children's empowerment.

The concept of play in this book comes from a particular perspective underpinned by playwork principles which recognise children's 'capacity for positive development, enhanced through access to the broadest range of environments and play opportunities' (Playwork Principles Scrutiny Group, 2005; Brown, 2008). Play is viewed from a child-directed perspective, supporting children in having a degree of freedom in the choices and decisions they make as they play. Enabling children to have a sense of autonomy in their play through controlling what, how, when and who they play with is seen as supporting their participation, ownership and ability to express themselves through a process of empowerment.

The subject of children's play has been extensively explored, from studies of the function of play amongst animals (Huizinga, 1955) to developmental and therapeutic functions of play. It has been characterised as an exertion of excess energy (Spencer, 1820–1903); a cathartic process (Hall, 1846–1924); a key part of cognitive development (Piaget, 1951); a potentially self-healing process (Axline, 1964) and a reflection of culture and evolutionary drive (Hughes, 2001). Yet play is a complex construction that cannot be encapsulated simply in a single overarching definition; its very nature includes some or all of the characteristics outlined above, depending on the way in which it is interpreted within the context of a situation. Conceptually, definitions of play must necessarily concern children's 'own activity: a voluntary, intrinsically motivated experience where the activity itself is more important than the outcome' (Bateson, 2005, p. 14).

Moyles (2010) aligns defining play with seizing bubbles and argues that play can be recognised without the need for a precise definition. However contemporary understandings of play in early childhood are wide ranging, from play as child-led and open-ended without following an adult agenda to structured, adult-directed activity. As use of the term 'play' encompasses such a broad ideological spectrum and multiple perspectives, this inevitably translates into a patchwork of professional practice in supporting children's opportunities to play. Furthermore, in any one setting, even though the opportunities offered are ostensibly the same for all children, play is such a personal experience that while one child may appear to be having fun, another may not have the same experience when playing in a similar situation. Howard and McInnes (2010) argue that when considering what play means to an individual child, it is important to make distinctions based on the emotional cues being given by that child, such as levels of fun and amount of choice, as well as considering the environmental cues such as the context and location of play. Again, this means that considering play from a child's perspective may provide indicators to recognising what is and what is not play, although this is not necessarily given weight in the various discourses of play.

Discourses of social play

Discourse relates to a body of thinking where groups of individuals share the same language when talking about a topic and develop shared understanding around different perspectives. Foucault (1972) believed discourse is also connected to emotional responses and therefore can develop and change depending on feelings and experiences at different points in life. Discourse also relates to professional practice informing daily activities, the way in which working with children is approached and how thinking and reflecting on practice becomes part of an individual's value and belief system (Albon, 2010). In a perhaps unconscious way, a dominant discourse can influence thinking, behaviour and practice towards topics such as children's play. Some groups have power to enforce their discourse more than others, for example government views of the purpose of education may hold more influence than a community action group promoting the need for children's play spaces. However, although government views may be more widely disseminated, they may not necessarily carry more weight at a local level. Consequently the power of dominant discourses can shape wider understanding through 'regimes of truth' (Foucault cited in Rabinow, 1984), whereby a particular discourse shapes thinking and debate. Different practice, values and beliefs are developed depending on the discourse adopted, but this usually happens on an unconscious level rather than being a deliberate decision. Equally, discourses can overlap where there are some shared commonalities of practice based on different understanding or slightly different perspectives. Van Oers (2010) argues that historically play has been based on two assumptions: that play originates from natural behaviour, grounded in naturalistic interpretation of human development, which has been romanticised by the writings of pioneers such as Rousseau; and alternatively that play is separate to learning or work, where children practice or simulate skills in preparation for adulthood. Ailwood (2003) takes this further by outlining three dominant discourses of play: the romantic or nostalgic discourse; the play characteristic discourse; and the developmental discourse. Each discourse considers the value and understanding of play from different perspectives, resulting in different approaches to play in contemporary early childhood practice.

Romantic or nostalgic discourse

The nostalgic discourse of play views childhood as a state of innocence and play as 'natural'. This discourse has its roots in the Romantic era and the writing of people such as Rousseau (1712–1778), Pestalozzi (1747–1827) and Froebel (1782–1852). A nostalgic discourse can idealise childhood play experiences, and adults who uphold this view reflect on their own play as a child and remember its positive aspects such as excitement and freedom. The nostalgic discourse attracts an emotive response such that adults reflecting on their own play experiences want to provide similar positive experiences for their own children or children in their care to those that they encountered as a child. Consequently, when discussing play, adherents of the nostalgic discourse often use an anecdote or story where what is being remembered is positive and reflects the romantic notion of the benefits of play.

The nostalgic discourse of play has been the dominant discourse until fairly recently (Ailwood, 2003). This has meant that play has not always been recognised as a rich environment for learning or having the potential for holistic development. The nostalgic discourse has allowed play to be compartmentalised as something that happens after a more formal, adult-directed activity. The latter is usually prioritised because the learning potential of this type of activity can be analysed in a more systematic way. The term 'just playing' sums up the notion of play as a by-product of children, something that happens after completing formal activities (Moyles, 1989). Thus, a nostalgic view does not always recognise the inherent value of the processes of play, as it focuses on the emotional significance of play as described in individual recollections of positive past experiences.

Play characteristic discourse

In contrast, researchers who uphold the play characteristic discourse (Bruce, 2011) attempt to identify different behaviours evident in children's play and group them together into categories that can be used to support further analysis and discussion. Underlying the play characteristic discourse is the assumption that the various categories of play can be described as a set of processes rather than outcomes or as an end in itself (for example, Bekoff and Byers, 1981; Martin and Caro, 1985; Pellegrini and Smith, 2005; Hughes, 2001). The categories can be conceptualised as making up the different 'ingredients' of play and offer an explanatory framework that can be used to understand the behaviours that contribute to play in different situations. In providing an operational definition of each category of play they identify, there is an attempt to differentiate between categories in terms of what children are doing and what this means for their development.

This research enterprise has resulted in extensive categorisations with long lists of play types. For instance, Blatchford et al. (1990) name 24 different play types based on Opie and Opie's (1969) definitions of children's games played on streets and playgrounds, and Hughes (2006) identifies 16 types of play among children in his playwork research. Ailwood (2003, p. 289), however, critiques this approach and argues that lists of play characteristics are a 'conglomerate of various constructions and discourses of childhood' and that play characteristics should not be seen in isolation but within the context of social and cultural influences. In practice, the play characteristic discourse is used to label and describe what happens in children's play as a way of supporting early childhood educators in recognising characteristics of play. For example, Garvey (1991) identifies five commonly accepted characteristics of play: positive affect, intrinsic motivation, free choice, active engagement, and as the made up world or fantasy of children. Labelling play characteristics in this way means that their definitions are open to subjective interpretation which supports debate amongst the early childhood community to continually evolve and develop shared understanding.

Howard (2002) considers play in terms of sets of criteria or continuum definitions, which focus on behaviours and dispositions of play. She argues that the different sets of criteria for defining play all have the same thing in common, that they are based on adults looking at, and making subjective judgements based on, the observable act of play. In the same way as Garvey (1991), Howard points out that what is observed is open to interpretation and the same sequence of play may be viewed or characterised in different ways by different adult observers.

Developmental discourse

The developmental discourse of play not only focuses on cognitive aspects of play, but also the benefits of play for social, emotional and physical development. Vygotsky (1978) believed that play is a central part of children's development and play behaviour is a way in which a child can practice existing skills and acquire new ones. This discourse recognises that much of children's play is social and relies on interaction with other children. Duncan and Tarulli (2003) argue that through play children develop relationships and become conscious of themselves through, and because of, the actions and reactions other children display towards them. Consequently play contributes to children developing an understanding of who they are and how their personality is perceived by others. Vygotsky (1966) considers that play is a 'leading activity' for children because in play children demonstrate their understanding of social roles, social rules and aspects of social organisation. Children play within the boundaries of their knowledge, but then also use play to push those boundaries, experiment with ideas and discover new ways of doing things. Vygotsky (1966) recognises that although play may not be the predominant activity for preschool children it is a leading source of development. He states, 'the child moves forward essentially through play activity' (Vygotsky, 1966, p. 16). Vygotsky also acknowledges the affective drive of play that allows children's imagination to be linked to developing confidence within a play situation. He suggests that confidence could also be developed more generally through mastery of a skill or task.

According to Vygotsky, the potential of play for cognitive development lies in the way that it can suspend reality and liberate children from the immediate constraints of real-life situations; opening opportunities to explore pretend characters or objects: 'As in the focus of a magnifying glass, play contains all developmental tendencies in a condensed form and is itself a major source of development' (Vygotsky, 1978, p. 102). Finally, he believes that for very young children, the motivation to play is not intrinsic, but created from cultural influences, dependent upon adult guidance (Vygotsky, 1978). The influence of culture and social interaction in all contexts of play is widely acknowledged as significant, however, the belief that children are not intrinsically motivated to play is a contested view.

Children's intrinsic motivation for play

Hughes (2001) argues that the essence of play is based on children's intrinsic desire and curiosity. He believes that play is something that children have to do and can be evidenced through children's interactions with different opportunities and their motivation to use those opportunities to satisfy their curiosity. In a similar way,

Moyles (2005) considers that children are neither in nor out of play, but are more or less playing in different degrees at all times and Sutton Smith (1997) views play as a lifelong activity that can occur at any age.

The concept of intrinsic motivation for play is also underpinned by playwork principles, which recognise children's 'capacity for positive development, enhanced through access to the broadest range of environments and play opportunities' (Playwork Principles Scrutiny Group, 2005; Brown, 2008). Play is viewed from a self-motivated, child-directed perspective, supporting children in having a degree of freedom in the choices and decisions they make as they play. Enabling children to have a sense of autonomy in their play through controlling what, how, when and who they play with is seen as supporting their motivation to participate, take ownership in a situation and explore different ways to express themselves.

Hughes (2001) explains this further through arguing that play has two main interlocking characteristics. The first is that play has an immediate impact on the children involved. It is something that they engage in to make sense of their own situation and the context they are in. The reasoning for play may not always be apparent to onlookers or indeed for other children involved in the same play, but Hughes identifies that this can be attributed to play being intrinsically motivated where children have a desire to play. Moyles (2005, p. 3) agrees that children have a 'natural inclination to play alongside a natural instinct to learn and be curious and inventive'. The second characteristic is that play has a wider influence, which is a transpersonal characteristic. A play experience can impact on what children are feeling or doing 'in the moment' but also relates to what has happened in the past, where children draw on previous experiences to inform what they are doing in their play. Children's experiences may also inform how they play in the future; triggering reactions based on previous play encounters. Therefore recognising and implementing play at the centre of all early childhood practice can support developing a play 'history' for children, built on play memories, which can be recreated or revisited at a later date.

Child-directed or child-centred play allows children a sense of autonomy, controlling what they do, how they do it and when to stop or change their play. Creating an ethos based on following children's ideas and motivations requires educators to trust children and value their play. Child-directed play can be unpredictable and giving children a say in what they do means someone has to listen, take on board what children say and be prepared to respond sensitively and appropriately (Canning, 2012). Consequently, educators who place play at the centre of practice need to be flexible in their approach and facilitate a space that allows play to develop in a way that the child intends. The wealth of insights into a child's individual qualities and experiences that play can generate should not be underestimated. These considerations form the basis for recognising that children have a capacity for developing ways of seeing the world, problem-solving, learning and developing 'meaning making' in their play.

An important aspect of supporting play is to recognise children's choices and reflect on why those choices have been made. Listening to children's views is vital in establishing a child-centred environment. However, Greene and Hill (2005, p. 18) identify that 'it is important not to just pay lip-service to the idea of listening to children or exploiting what is learnt from children about their lives in ways that meet the adult agenda only'. Consequently educators need to be aware, not just about how they listen to children, but also to be clear about the rationale for advocating children's autonomy and voice.

Recognition of the right to play

Children's play has become recognised as a right in itself and is formally set out in Article 31 of the United Nations Convention on the Rights of the Child (UNCRC), which states: 'Parties recognise the right of the child to rest and leisure, to engage in play and recreational activities appropriate to the age of the child and to participate freely in cultural life and the arts' (United Nations, 1989, Article 31, part 1). 'Parties shall respect and promote the right of the child to participate fully in cultural and artistic life and shall encourage the provision of appropriate and equal opportunities for cultural, artistic, recreational and leisure activity' (United Nations, 1989, Article 31, part 2).

Davey and Lundy (2011) argue that a rights-based approach to children's play emphasises matters such as freedom, choice and inclusion and that these issues are an important and necessary part of children's play. The intrinsic value of play for children and the significance of adult free play spaces advocated by Hughes (2001) emphasises that play is important in its own right. Davey and Lundy (2011) go as far to say that play is an entitlement, not an optional luxury to be fitted in around planned activities.

Considering children's play from a rights-based approach means that what children do within their play is also significant. Participation in play is a way of developing interaction and communication between children which in turn supports the construction and creation of social relationships (Prout and James, 1997). Children's voice within play enables them to have their ideas listened to by other children, to make decisions about their involvement in social group play and show their choices through their physical contribution or emotional investment. Having ownership of their own play is also significant for children; it supports their active engagement in contributing and influencing what is happening and potentially taking a lead in the development of play.

The importance of children's participation, voice and ownership in play situations is supported by Articles 12 and 13 of the UNCRC. Article 12 declares that 'children who are capable of forming their own views have the right to express those views freely in all matters that affect them' (United Nations, 1989, Article 12, part 1). A play situation is where potentially children have the most influence over other children in what they are doing and whom they are playing with. Article 13 presents the right to freedom of expression and specifically details the range of media that should be open to children to receive information and to express their ideas either 'orally, in writing or in print, in the form of art or through any other

The significance of play and empowerment 25

media of the child's choice' (United Nations, 1989, Article 13, part 1). As Powell (2009) points out, in early childhood settings play is usually the medium of choice for children to express their ideas.

In this example Amy demonstrates her play skills and motivation as she creates a story around her small world toys and Lego bricks.

Intrinsic motivation: Amy's need to create a dragon

Amy is at home and has a box with Lego bricks and small world figures tipped out in front of her. She is arranging the small world figures in a semi-circle and uses the bricks to make a dragon (see Figure 2.1). She is talking to herself as she builds the shape of the creature and warns her small world figures that 'a dragon is coming!' She concentrates on what she is doing and is immersed in finding the blocks she wants to create the dragon whilst extending her imaginary play by talking to the figures and creating scenarios of what they might do when the dragon comes.

The video sequence is 1 minute and 58 seconds long. The decision to time the video sequences is explained in the previous chapter where the children and settings that took part in the research were introduced. Under each of the time codes in Table 2.1 a short description of what happened in the video is explained.

FIGURE 2.1 Amy creating her dragon

TABLE 2.1 Description and time codes of Amy's play

Focus child	Amy
Location of video clip	Home
Total length of video clip	01.58.38

Timing	Description
00.01.10–00.20.30	Amy is sat on the floor in the living room and tips out Lego bricks and small world figures from a box. She starts to sort out the small world figures and stands them in a semi-circle next to her.
00.21.12–00.35.16	She selects Lego bricks and begins to put them together. She is humming quietly to herself as she is doing this.
00.48.02–01.05.32	Amy announces to the small world figures that she is building a dragon. She says, 'He has got a long neck, look, and he is going to have fire so watch out!'
01.08.10–01.20.30	Amy continues to concentrate on building the shape of her dragon, struggling to snap the pieces of Lego together. She doesn't ask for any help, but uses her tummy to brace the bricks against her so she can use two hands to push the pieces together.
01.30.16–01.52.36	'Nearly there', she says to the figures. When she is satisfied with the dragon she makes a roaring sound and knocks the figures down with her creation.

Being able to express views and to be in a position of control or ownership of play enhances skills such as decision-making, communication and negotiation which Sinclair and Franklin (2000) consider as part of the process of empowering children so that they have a sense of self-efficacy and the experience of positive self-esteem. The process of empowerment goes beyond just recognising children's rights; the right to play has value in supporting children with opportunities to express themselves on their own terms, to explore their own interests and to recognise their limits and boundaries. Therefore it is important to encourage children to have choices, explore materials, as Amy is doing, and also environments, emotions and social relationships (Mason and Bolzan, 2010).

The nature of empowerment

The term 'empowerment', a bit like 'play', is ambiguous, defined in subtly different ways depending on the discipline or profession in which it is used. In this book empowerment is examined in relation to children's social play. It is explored within child-initiated play contexts which give children the opportunity to make choices and decisions with their peers.

Defining children's empowerment is challenging because although the term is shared in many disciplines, how empowerment is understood and what happens in practice can be very different. Being empowered is often assumed, yet difficult to define in action because it can also be expected to manifest itself in different ways, depending on the context of the situation and who is involved. Rappaport (1984) argues that it is problematic as a generic term because it encompasses a range of emotions and behaviours suggesting an intangible and elusive concept. For example, he suggests that empowerment can operate on an individual level or can be experienced by a group. It may be seen in changes in behaviour through actions and interactions in social situations and through the way in which connections are made between people, such as finding out that they share common interests. Page and Czuba (1999) suggest that being empowered is part of a more complex process involving individual emotions where not everyone may feel empowered at the same time or take the same route to finding a sense of empowerment.

The concept of empowerment is an area of interest in other professions such as community development, economics, youth work and education but is used in different ways to understand behaviour and actions in different contexts. Within these professions there is general caution in pursuing a definition of empowerment in case it becomes prescriptive or formulaic, contradicting the very nature of empowerment as a holistic concept encompassing an experience or way of being (Zimmerman, 1984; Gomm, 1993; Rivera and Tharp, 2006).

Ashcroft (1987) agrees that empowerment should be seen more as a process rather than something that is achieved. He views empowerment as an enabling process where experiences can be made possible for children through the opportunities they have, and by establishing a support network that nurtures children's self-belief, competence and confidence. According to this argument children who regularly encounter empowering experiences believe in their own capability and will engage with others equipped with a positive attitude resulting in positive outcomes. Ashcroft (1987) argues that the process of empowerment involves a number of components: individual reactions and interactions with others; the environment or context of the experience; and others' involvement and responses in supporting an empowering experience.

Bonnel and Lindon (2000, p. 280) define empowerment as 'conferring power to an individual through an enabling or facilitating process', however understanding who has power in different play situations and considering how they use that power is also central to the concept of an empowering process. This is because children may experience empowerment or dis-empowerment in play as a result of their responses to other children and to their surrounding environment. These experiences may not only support children's exploration of their interests, but also contribute to their experience of empowerment if they are positive or dis-empowerment if they are negative. James and James (2004) suggest that children shape their childhood experiences within the conditions available to them. Therefore, in a social play context, empowerment may be explained by focusing on the ways in which children use their relationships with others through their participation, expression of voice and the way in which they use the environment and resources to influence the context they are involved in. For example, they may do this by using a resource in a particular way to encourage other children to copy or join in; they may persuade other children to change their play to meet their own agenda; or be creative in their environment so that they have ownership of play through perhaps leading and including other children to share a play experience. Again, close observation is needed in order to establish the parameters of social play that supports empowerment.

This book focuses on children's reactions and interactions with their peers in social play situations. It also considers the impact of the environment in supporting children's choices and decisions through participation with their peers, the way they express themselves through their verbal and non-verbal communication and through their capacity to have ownership of their play. Making a judgement about children's empowering experiences involves assessing not only the components Ashcroft identifies, but also the characteristics displayed in play, such as imaginative or creative play. This means that accurate observation and interpretation of the apparent nature and purpose of children's play is pivotal in deciding what characteristics or processes of a play situation are empowering or dis-empowering.

Summary

This chapter has explored the complexities of play and considered the most common discourses of play. Intrinsic motivation as a basis for play has been argued, coupled with the right of children to have opportunities to play. These opportunities support exploration and discovery not only in social play, but also in situations where children play on their own, creating their own worlds and imaginary play. As with play, the notion of empowerment is also ambiguous yet both terms are complementary in relation to the way in which they afford children opportunities for following their own interests. Throughout the following chapters the interplay between empowerment and play is explored, determining how the process of empowerment is supported through play.

3

THE POWER OF PLAY

This chapter provides a review of literature relating to the complex nature of power relationships and dynamics in children's play. The power dynamics between children are explored as well as how adults influence children's choices and decisions without necessarily realising or meaning to. The chapter argues for children's right to play, focusing on pedagogical approaches to play and how play is interpreted in everyday practice. In this way the culturally and socially situated nature of power relationships is made evident.

The early childhood educator's role is explored in relation to supporting children's play opportunities and experiences. A central aspect of this is reflective practice where shared understanding about play and supporting children through play is continually questioned and evaluated. Being aware of the power relationships that exist is vital to the process of reflection and understanding the complex discourses that exist, and why they exist, in children's play. The chapter concludes with a definition of empowerment which forms the basis for the analysis and interpretation of the subsequent chapters.

A sociocultural perspective

A sociocultural perspective in relation to power relationships emphasises the interdependence between cultural contexts and social interaction in developing knowledge and understanding. Vygotsky (1978) argues that all human activity is motivated by, and takes place in, cultural contexts that are developed through the ways in which people communicate and their actions towards each other. He argues that each individual holds a personal cultural connection or history that shapes their thinking, values and beliefs. Individuals' thinking processes are expressed consciously and unconsciously when interacting with others and exchanging views. Therefore individuals develop an understanding of who they are, where they have come from, (i.e. their family history) and what they believe in within a specific cultural context. Thus, cultural understanding and influences are created, maintained and perpetuated through expectations and experiences passed on from generation to generation. Rogoff (2003, p. 368) argues that 'culture is not just something other people do, but is about understanding our own cultural heritage, perspectives and beliefs as well as being open to a consideration of the needs of people with contrasting backgrounds'.

Within different social and cultural contexts there are common practices that occur based on unquestioned assumptions about how things are done or roles that different people occupy. Corsaro (2005) suggests that these assumptions shape children's cultural understanding and influence their contribution to the adult world. Common or taken-for-granted practices are often reaffirmed through actual experiences, for example, what has been seen or heard or emphasised through pictures or stories. Therefore, how children relate to the world is largely a function based on what they know of their own cultural context and the influence of wider societal norms (Greene and Hill, 2005). Through drawing on a sociocultural perspective, children should be viewed as active participants in their communities although it is clear that they are affected and influenced by the decisions and practices of adults. Nevertheless, children are also viewed as being able to influence what matters to them through their actions and through being offered the opportunity for their opinion and views to count (James and James, 2004). Children's position within society, therefore, can change as their community changes or thinking develops. For this reason, Rogoff (2003) views sociocultural theory as something that constantly evolves as society changes.

Power relationships in play

Assumptions about social and cultural contexts shape children's knowledge and understanding and influence their contribution to the adult world. Within any given situation, anyone can have the opportunity to be powerful through their actions and reactions (MacNaughton, 2005). Power can be productive, influencing dynamics between adults and children, and between children at different times and in different situations. Deleuze (1993) argues that power is determined between two separate forces and emerges when one force acts over the other. Therefore power is influenced by interactions and alters in intensity depending on the situation in which it is used.

Both Foucault (1980) and Deleuze discuss how power is not static. Deleuze focuses on the *affect* of power and how a person may be able to think or act differently when they feel powerful. He suggests that an individual can be influential as well as influenced. Within the context of play, situations may offer opportunities for children to experience the affect of being powerful as well as being powerless. The ability to be creative and play out different scenarios supports what Olsson (2009) argues as capacities that can be created and imagined.

Children gain a sense of power by being given the opportunity to make choices in play and to act on their decisions (Nugin et al., 2016). The process of supporting children to feel in control of their play requires a gradual development of trust on the part of adults in what children will choose to do, and an understanding of how play can be facilitated to ensure a safe and stimulating environment. Social group play interactions that children encounter help them to practice and develop their understanding of the patterns and processes that underpin social relationships and friendship. Therefore power dynamics is a process dependent upon the interaction between children and adults and is negotiated through relationships and dialogue (Hoyle, 1999).

Truths

Having power over others can produce a set of 'truths' which groups of individuals start to believe in (Gore, 1993). But Albon (2010) warns that power can never be value free or objective and as such the motivation for power should always be questioned. A set of truths believed and practised by individuals within a given profession creates a 'regime of truth' which in time becomes an authoritative consensus about how things should be done. Gore (1993) believes that developing a regime of truth helps establish power relations. But Foucault views truth as an 'art of government' where government refers to 'techniques and procedures for directing human behaviour' (Rabinow, 1984, p. 81). Consequently, Foucault identifies that truths become woven together to govern what is accepted as a way of doing something, or a goal to strive for, or a way to act, think or feel.

Within early childhood there are many perspectives of what children's play should look like, its content and purpose, which are held as 'truths'. If a particular truth of children's play is part of daily practice, it becomes part of what that individual does, thinks or feels and is embedded in actions and reactions to children's needs. Practice then disseminates through the setting and influences others, which results in a particular 'truth' being accepted. This results in the governability of groups of people where they are compliant in being told what to do and how to do it. In this way power can operate without people realising it, resulting in an undercurrent of practices and relationships which may influence children's experiences within a setting.

Adult–child power dynamics

Adults consciously and unconsciously hold power over children's play, making decisions which impact on children's choices. The physical environment provides boundaries for children, as does how educators and other children behave within that space. Most situations that children encounter have a set of rules which help to organise and guide behaviour and children learn that stepping outside of the rules means there will be consequences. Ailwood (2010) argues that from a very young age children understand how social rules work based on their own experiences and by observing other children and adults in a range of situations. Children can recognise when they are able to push the boundaries and Loizou (2005) suggests that there are times when children are empowered by the idea of 'seeing what might happen if ...', causing a reaction from an educator or parent/carer. Foucault (1980) suggests that power operates on a fluid basis, so that one person is not powerful all of the time. In this way power can be productive, influencing different relationships between adults and children and between children at different times and in different situations.

When educators work in well-established routines they may become complacent and lose sight of providing different opportunities for children to express their individuality. Consequently Howard (2010) warns that educators should be mindful of the power that 'top down' external influences may have over them through policy and curriculum guidance in directing practice. Foucault refers to this as 'governmentality', where groups of people are managed through being told what to do and how to do it (cited in Rabinow, 1984). But power may also exist in knowledge, and understanding the power that individuals hold through their experience and knowledge base of early childhood cannot be underestimated, as MacNaughton states: 'Once we understand how power operates through ideologies to oppress and constrain in our particular social and political contexts, we can begin to understand what needs to change and why' (MacNaughton, 2005, p. 11).

Are children in charge?

Children sometimes test out the boundaries of power relationships in their interactions with educators and parents or other adults (Loizou, 2005). Children making decisions about what they are going to do or how they are going to behave, act consciously through what Foucault (1980) describes as disciplinary power where children are able to self-regulate their own behaviour or make a decision not to follow instruction. It is clear that the everyday rules that children encounter and learn through their interactions with others may generate a sense of normality through regulating expectations and accepting hierarchical structures (Alverson, 2002). Similarly, children learn that different structures and procedures exist in different situations; as Loizou (2005) observes, children often direct each other or may even reverse conventional power relationships. For example, they may remind an educator or parent/carer about what they should be doing next or about rules associated with certain play such as wearing an apron when painting. Knowing the rules can offer children a sense of power and familiarity, supporting a confidence in their actions and interactions with others.

This next example considers the power dynamics between Harry and his friends (all four years old) and Harry's mother when they are outside in the forest school at a 'stay and play' event. The children's centre that Harry attends holds weekly 'stay and play' sessions where parents bring their children to explore the forest school environment. Parents stay and chat while an early childhood educator leads a semi-structured session. She introduces a topic and then facilitates children to explore that topic further or to simply explore the forest environment and follow their own interests.

Power dynamics: Harry and the rain water

Harry and his three friends are sitting under a large plastic sheet suspended by rope tied to nearby trees (see Figure 3.1). They are near the fire pit in the middle of the

FIGURE 3.1 Playing with dripping water

woodland area that is used as a meeting point. It is the beginning of the session and the children are waiting to be told they can go and play. Close by, Harry's mother is chatting to other mothers who have brought their children to the session. The educator is busy, chatting to other parents and welcoming children.

Under each of the time codes in Table 3.1 a short description of what happened in the video is explained.

Through video stimulated review (Forman, 1999) both Harry's mother and the educator watched the video back a few days later. Harry's mother commented:

> At the time it was naughty, he was letting the water in. But looking at it again I can see the fun side of it and he wasn't doing anything wrong at all for me to get worked up about really, to tell him to stop really. So that was quite funny, to see me and my reaction to something there. But to look at it from his point of view it was just a bit of fun.

The educator focused on Harry when reviewing the video and commented:

> It was quite funny watching that because it was like Harry was more in control of what was going on, the other were following Harry there and he wasn't afraid to break the 'rules', he seemed more confident and tried to push the boundaries his mum was setting!

TABLE 3.1 Description and time codes of Harry's play

Focus child	Harry
Location of video clip	Children's centre: outside
Total length of video clip	02.05.32

Timing	Description
00.01.05–00.18.30	It is raining. Harry and his friends are under the plastic sheet to stay out of the rain, but the water is dripping off the side of the sheet onto the ground. Harry puts his hand out to catch the drips. He lets out squeals of excitement which attracts the attention of the other boys. They come over to him and copy his actions, trying to catch the drips.
00.19.20–00.42.02	Harry sees the rope that is holding up the plastic sheet. He gives it a tug. This makes the rain water that had been pooling on the top of the sheet run down the side. The children's arms get wet. There are more squeals of delight and Harry starts to rub the water up and down his arms.
00.43.11–01.05.16	Harry's mother hears the commotion and shouts across to Harry to behave. Harry ignores her and continues to catch the drips in one hand, whilst tugging on the rope with the other. No more water falls, but the sheet has loosened and is flapping in the wind.
01.06.20–01.32.45	Harry's mother comes over the boys, she says: 'What have I told you Harry?' Harry giggles and the other boys move slightly away Harry tugs on the rope again. 'Do it one more time Harry, one more time …' Harry goes to tug the rope. His mother grabs his arm, 'No! What have I told you?'
01.33.14–02.05.32	Harry pulls away and moves to the other side of the shelter. Harry's mum is distracted by another parent. She points a finger at him as if to say 'no more'. The boys huddle in the corner and tentatively start to put their hands out again, catching the drips of water.

In this example, Harry wants to play with the water but is aware of his mother's desire for him to stop. He is testing the boundaries in his play but also self-regulating what he is doing so that he doesn't get into any more trouble. His mother makes a decision about how she is going to handle the situation and reverts to being motivated by perceived 'good' behaviour through the structures she considers to be appropriate, i.e. not playing with the plastic sheet and making the water fall on the other children and surrounding area. Waller (2005) argues that play experiences offered to children often reflect a socially constructed view of childhood of what is considered appropriate at the time. In this context, the outdoor play environment is considered suitable, yet the actions and reactions from Harry are not. The power lies with the adult, as expectations of how Harry and his friends play are enforced rather than supporting their exploration.

It is a skill to judge the flexibility needed to meet the curiosity of children and give them opportunities to experience different resources, make choices and express preference over what they are doing through their play (Brunson and Vogt, 1996). Adults have a greater awareness of social and cultural traditions and therefore are not only able to impose these on children through behavioural expectations but are also able to assert a disproportionate aspect of power over children because they can control the environment and what happens in it (Ernst, 2014). In the example, Harry's mother warned him of unspoken consequences, which presumably she knew Harry would understand. She adopted an authoritative position without fully engaging in what Harry and his friends were doing. A snapshot of his actions prompted a sanctioning response, power that Harry's mother felt she had because of her relationship with her son. She accepted the context of what Harry was doing at face value, 'he was doing something naughty' and her response was to stop it.

Harry also held power in this situation, however, and he used his interaction with other children to continue his game regardless of his mother's warning. He used the physical space to move away from her as much as he could so he could continue catching the drips of water. Hughes (1996) suggests that 'both the content and intent of play should be determined by the child' and that play should be 'child-empowering' (pp. 22–23). Harry demonstrated through his play that he was able to do what he wanted to do, i.e. catching the drips and exploring the feeling of the water on his arms regardless of what his mother wanted him to do. He was powerful in his own situation through continuing to make choices and explore his interests. He was able to sustain his participation with his friends through negotiating the space, avoiding bringing further attention to what he was doing. Treseder (1997) suggests that active engagement with other children enables them to take part on their own terms. Harry was perhaps more confident to continue to play with the water because his friends were there than if he had been on his own. The social situation contributed to him having power in that context to defy his mother's wishes. Therefore it is important to consider the social implications of empowerment and the influence that change within and outside a community can have on the process of being empowered.

An empowering community

The way that communities facilitate empowering experiences is significant in fostering children's socialisation, participation and engagement in everyday activities so that these skills are practised and continue to develop during play (Rivera and Tharp, 2006). The idea that empowerment can become solely focused on the individual, whilst ignoring the social dimensions which support the structures and processes surrounding empowerment, is inconceivable according to social work author To (2009). Jiang et al. (2011) argue that there is a need to find a balance between focusing on empowering individuals and empowering a group of people and that both need to be taken into consideration and work together to energise individuals and to create collective responses in supporting the overall process of empowerment.

Underlying power relationships that exist between individuals, social contexts and the wider community are significant in understanding how empowering processes can be sustained. Page and Czuba (1999) argue that both individuals and communities need to be open to change and that if power is static, consistently held by one or the other, then empowerment is not conceivable in a meaningful way. Power can expand or be shared, based on common experiences and individuals coming together to achieve a goal or to make something happen.

Change is also a key element in the argument that empowerment is generated from within a community. The professional community considered as the 'early childhood sector' has experienced many changes over the last decade with a workforce that has been required to adapt on a regular basis, but change can be unsettling and is often seen as a *dis*-empowering experience. Katz (1998) argues that if change is enforced through 'top-down' perspectives derived from political thinking and policy change then individuals may feel dis-empowered through the lack of engagement with the ideology or reasoning for change. She considers that only when individuals are involved in a 'bottom-up' approach can they become part of an empowering process. However, it is more complex because adopting new practices or changing existing ones requires a significant shift in adults' thinking and conceptualising children's play and pedagogy (Ailwood, 2011). A web of power relations exists that provide complexity and ambiguity in thinking about how individuals, groups and communities are empowered and how they co-exist alongside each other in everyday practice.

Child–child power dynamics

Bauman and May (2001) suggest children gain a sense of power by being given the opportunity to make choices in play and to act on their decisions. The process of supporting children to feel in control of their play requires a gradual development of trust on the part of educators in what children will choose to do, and an understanding of how play can be facilitated to ensure an environment that is safe but stimulating. Bandura (1962) stresses the importance of supporting children in building a sense of self-efficacy where through different experiences they develop self-belief about their effectiveness and competence. Developing these attitudes enables children to cope with particular situations. According to Bandura, the play interactions that children encounter in social group play help them to practice and develop their understanding of the patterns and processes that underpin social relationships and friendship. In the same way, Ashcroft (1987) views power as a potential capability that is exercised through action and thus as a process rather than as an end product. Power is subsequently sustained through relationships, dialogue and negotiation. For children, it is reasonable to suppose that these processes feature strongly in social play and so this kind of play allows children to experience empowerment.

In social group play where children have choice it may be particularly revealing to observe the decisions they make in terms of their engagement depending on how self-assured they feel to actively participate (Canning, 2011). This is because, as Smith (2010) suggests, when children make play choices they can use the opportunity to make decisions about their engagement and behaviour. They can then be innovative in their thinking and apply this to their play situation to develop strategies to be accepted into social group play (Smith, 2010). Children involved, for example, in risky play have to find the courage within themselves to take risks such as climbing a tree or acting independently of their peers, but in demonstrating their confidence to other children they often become leaders of the play, being able to influence other children into copying their actions and behaviour (Sandseter, 2009). This corresponds with Foucault's positioning of power as an action rather than a possession which can be supported through different relationships at different times (Foucault, 1980).

Pedagogy

The positioning of play in the curriculum and how play informs pedagogical practices is central in reflecting on power dynamics. Pramling Samuelsson and Carlsson (2008, p. 623) argue that 'play and learning are natural components of children's everyday lives' and should be a seamless way of nurturing children's development. Ambiguous terms are used to describe play, and the challenge is to be able to clearly articulate what happens in practice and defend decisions in relation to curriculum demands (Stephen, 2010). In England the Early Years Foundation Stage (EYFS) states that 'children learn by leading their own play and by taking part in play which is guided by adults' (Department for Education (DfE), 2014, p. 9). However, it does not provide any guidance on desirable pedagogic practice to support play other than 'it is expected that the balance will gradually shift towards more activities led by adults, to help children prepare for more formal learning, ready for year 1' (DfE, 2014, p. 9). Play does not fit easily within curricula which expect outcomes and the ability to measure children's progress because, as Wood (2010) argues, play is linked to wider benefits and determining factors such as physical and mental health, creativity and emotional well-being. Play is promoted within curriculum guidance as having a purpose, having a structure and reaching a satisfactory conclusion (DfE, 2014). Curriculum is usually compartmentalised into areas of learning, rather than adopting a holistic approach to children's experiences and learning.

The motivation for play is universal and intrinsic in children and is not bound by curricula, socio-economic status or class, as we explored in Chapter 2. Play is not about meeting political agendas or ticking the boxes for policy compliance, it is about children's experiences and how they are empowered by those experiences. However, educators work within a social and political context and often find themselves constrained by directives, reports, recommendations, guidance and requirements. Government policies also have a strategic impact not only in shaping early childhood provision but also in influencing what children should learn and the type of care and education that they should receive. This may have an impact on children's play within a setting if play is side-lined for other activities perceived as more important because they are highlighted by a curriculum. Yet all early childhood settings make some provision for play and children find opportunities for play, even if it is perhaps not the focus of the activity. Hughes (2001) maintains that all children find ways to play because it is something that they have to do as well as wanting to play and engage with others in play. He also argues that it is not just in organised settings where children play and these spaces, such as home environments, community play parks and street corners, also provide rich and diverse play experiences. Educators may feel overwhelmed by policy directives and curriculum demands and Howard and McInnes (2010) contest that this may have a detrimental effect on children's overall experience. They argue that maintaining a high level of reflective and knowledgeable practice is an adult and professional concern linked to professional identity and self-confidence. Professional identity and confidence, however, may be compromised where policy demands run counter to knowledge and experience.

The pedagogic strategy adopted by the early childhood educator is central to the play opportunities and power relationships children experience. Pedagogy has been described as the application of professional judgements enhancing the learning of another (Alexander, 2004) and the act of teaching (Watkins and Mortimer, 1999). In applying professional judgement, the educator makes decisions on the day-to-day routine of the early childhood setting, but as Moyles et al. (2002) warn, many educators are unaware that the everyday decisions they make have a pedagogical impact. Consequently there is a gap between 'acknowledging that play forms the bedrock of early learning' and 'an agreed pedagogy of play' (BERA, 2003, p. 14). Therefore, the pedagogical practice that exists in most early childhood practice is a historical mix of acknowledgement of the benefits of a play-based curriculum with the present emphasis on outcome-based learning strategies.

A pedagogical approach to play is based on how an educator frames pedagogy so that an ideology of 'playful approaches for successful outcomes' (DCSF, 2009, p. 4) can result in a balance between play which is child-centred and more formal adult-led activities which can extend children's learning. However Stephen (2010) argues that the challenge is that educators find it difficult to articulate how they support play-based learning and what pedagogy means on a personal and practice based level. Consequently the pedagogy of play is reduced to an instrument for learning rather than an activity that provides a transformative experience (Rogers, 2011).

In other cultures early childhood pedagogy is seen in a very different way. Reggio Emilia in Northern Italy is concerned with social construction of learning and meaning making involving the whole community and placing importance on hearing children's voices and acting on their opinions (Malaguzzi, 1998). The pedagogy adopted is a philosophy of practice where significance is placed on time for dialogue between children and space for social interaction. Children are co-constructors of knowledge and the adult role is to support the process. In Reggio Emilia the curriculum arises from children's interests and the pedagogic practice involves negotiating with children to understand what can be learnt from children's involvement with their peers and with the resources. The philosophy of practice is adopted by the whole community who it is hoped support every aspect of the process and act as a micro unit around the education of their children.

Across the other side of the world, the New Zealand curriculum, 'Te Whariki', also adopts a specific sociocultural perspective. Rather than content, the curriculum is based on nurturing learning dispositions through concentrating on developing children's well-being, belonging, contribution, communication and exploration (New Zealand Ministry of Education, 1996). Practitioners promote the different cultural heritage of Te Whariki (Maori and Western European) through activities, which encourage and support reciprocal and responsive relationships between children and between children and adults.

The role of the educator in both the examples of Reggio Emilia and New Zealand enables pedagogy where reflection on engagement between children and adults' engagement with children can be analysed as part of the play process. Taguchi (2010, p. 116) suggests that 'we must often stand back and wait to see what might happen next' and this approach supports a child-directed perspective with the role of the practitioner as having a 'hands off' approach.

Child-directed play supported by educators working within the Reggio Emilia and Te Whariki traditions highlights the importance of adopting a cultural historical perspective to the study of play and empowerment. This perspective recognises that views about the significance of play in children's everyday lives are dependent on the cultural context, historical traditions and cultural constructions of childhood prevalent in a particular society at any period in time. Mayall (2002) agrees and argues that childhood including play is informed by the culture of a surrounding community and therefore traditions, beliefs and values about childhood are shared and kept alive through generations of families and community connections. This is very much apparent in Reggio Emilia. Van Oers (2010, p. 196) recognises other influences in that 'the conception of play changes across history and cultures in compliance with specific historical, ideological and economic conditions', and this is reflected in the New Zealand example, where concerns about integration and Maori cultural heritage have had a significant influence on the early childhood curriculum.

Factors contributing to children's empowerment

Two main conclusions were drawn from a research project building on power dynamics and relationships that considered factors contributing to empowerment in play (Canning, 2011). To support the process of empowerment *human factors* focusing on the social and emotional investment needed by children to participate in play are required as well as *material factors* focusing on how children engage with the environment and resources available to them.

Human factors

The play behaviours associated with human factors supporting a process of empowerment include children taking risks, having their contributions valued and being able to express their views. For example, children may challenge themselves through pushing their physical limits or encourage other children to try something new in order to sustain a play situation. Ball et al. (2008) argue that children have an active appetite for risk and will seek out ways in which they test their physical boundaries. In taking risks, Gill (2007) suggests that children develop a better understanding of their physical environment and what they can achieve, giving them confidence to try something new or set themselves a challenge. Risk taking also motivates children to engage with other children, challenge themselves and access new experiences through determination to achieve their goals. Becoming involved in established social play is also an emotional risk children take in joining in for the first time or expressing their interest in case they are rejected by an established group of children. Neihart (1999) explains emotional risk as an individual and conscious decision to be in a position open to rejection and vulnerability. Emotional risk taking is sometimes more challenging to identify in young children's play because it is often understated and personal to the child (Ilardo, 1992). However it is potentially more rewarding if their risk is consequently repaid through being accepted and being able to participate in different play situations.

Taking an emotional risk also involves expressing opinions and although many children find this straightforward in play situations, having contributions valued by other children can be challenging, especially in a large group of children. Children can use a range of different modes of expression and communication with peers to show their preferences, but Buckley (2003) considers that both interactive and constructive actions from children are also important. This is because when children are engaged with their immediate surroundings they are focused and involved in play that helps them to develop their social awareness, listening and sharing skills. They are actively involved in play and co-constructing meaning from what they are doing.

Material factors

Material factors highlighted as significant for children's empowerment include the places and spaces where children play, the materials and equipment that are available to them, and using those materials in different and creative ways. Pramling Samuelsson and Carlsson (2008) argue that the context of children's experiences and how they make sense of what they are doing contributes to creative play experiences. Children have the capacity to adapt the resources and space they have to explore and experiment with ideas. Csikszentmihalyi (1997, p. 1) explains that 'creativity is a central source of meaning in our lives ... most of the things that are interesting, important and human are the results of creativity'. It is not surprising that the material factors of children's play are closely linked with creativity as it plays a central role in children's interactions with their environment, their peers and the different adults that they come into contact with. Children experiment with new thoughts and ideas and are curious to find out new things; they do this predominantly through playing with the resources available to them and exploring their environment. Jeffrey and Craft (2006) see children's engagement with creativity involving open adventures where children explore and develop knowledge and learning through trial and error. As a result, Sawyer (1997) considers children's play as a series of improvisations which are created on the spot and perpetuated by the interplay between children, their environment and resources.

The environment is central to children's play and Rogers (2000) argues that for any creativity to emerge it needs to be nourishing and nurturing, which promotes a culture of openness for new play opportunities to develop. The play environment supports children's exploration and curiosity allowing potential for following interests and experimenting with ideas. Rogers (2000) also suggests that connections are made while children play, stimulating opportunities for self-expression, problem-solving, communication and building social relationships. Play is about making meaningful connections and using ideas and resources in new ways. This not only supports sharing experiences with others, but widens children's ability to participate. Pramling Samuelsson and Carlsson (2008) agree that in play children find ways to symbolise and use objects that are meaningful to them. They argue that play puts a variety of demands on children, especially when they are engaged in a sustained form of creative play. For example, they have to remember what they have previously negotiated and what different objects and materials are supposed to be. This is where the human factors and material factors of play come together signifying that they are integrated and co-dependent.

Chapters 4 and 5 explore in detail the implications for empowerment in practice. However based on the arguments surrounding the power of play presented in this chapter and the ideology surrounding play and empowerment in Chapter 1, a definition of empowerment is useful to help understand the subsequent connections made between material and human factors influencing play. The definition takes into consideration the sociocultural influence and power relationships and dynamics that exist within children's play in different socio-economic contexts.

DEFINITION OF EMPOWERMENT

Empowerment in child-initiated, social play is not one single action, event or circumstance. It is concerned with examining individual choices and decisions based on social interactions, emotional responses and environmental influences within situated boundaries and resources. There are essential components that contribute to young children's experiences of empowerment; these are participation, voice and ownership.

Participation

The process of empowerment in child-initiated, social play is made up of interactions with other children which may influence the motivation or direction of play. How children decide to participate in play is significant. They may negotiate their way into a play situation, or be more assertive through taking the lead and instructing other children. They may challenge themselves through pushing their physical limits or encourage other children to try something new in order to sustain play. Children may use their initiative to change the game or focus of the play to ensure that it continues. Becoming involved in established social play is also an emotional risk children take in joining in for the first time or expressing their interest in case they are rejected by the group.

Voice

Empowerment in children's play also manifests itself through children expressing their point of view in agreement or opposition with others and using different modes of expression to show their preferences. This may be through making decisions about the materials or resources they want to play with, the space they want to play in or the timing of their play. Expressing an opinion amongst other children who also have opinions requires confidence and self-assurance, especially in a large social group. Through different ways of communicating with their peers, and having their opinions valued and heard by others, children are more willing to contribute their thoughts and ideas.

Ownership

Children want to feel that they are part of something, for example a family, an early childhood setting, or part of a wider community. When children have a sense of ownership they engage with and support other children through their actions and interest in what is happening around them. When children are able to engage with materials in different and creative ways, they have the opportunity to express independent thought and be able to follow it through to a conclusion of their own satisfaction. It is an emotive response of being included and a tangible experience of sharing something that has happened, been created or achieved together.

Articulating an informed and validated definition of empowerment for children's play brings together research based on child-initiated social play experiences explored in subsequent chapters. By stating the definition here, it gives an indication of what empowerment might look like in practice and helps to consider what might need to change to be able to implement empowerment in everyday situations.

Summary

This chapter has considered the power relationships that exist in children's play. Based on a sociocultural perspective, adult–child and child–child power dynamics have been explored. The example of Harry and the rain water highlights the complexities of power relationships and the reactions of both adults and children within an everyday interaction demonstrate how power can be fluid and influence subsequent actions. How power is influential in early childhood pedagogy is particularly significant in relation to the role of the educator and the position taken in supporting children's ability to be empowered. The human and material factors contributing towards empowerment, culminating in a definition of empowerment, are instrumental in building on knowledge and understanding throughout the subsequent chapters.

4
INDICATORS OF EMPOWERING PLAY BEHAVIOUR

This chapter brings together video observations of children's play and interviews with parents and educators. It explains key indicators of children's empowering play behaviour and acknowledges parents' and educators' opinions about children's play preferences. Adults' understandings of empowerment are weaved together to explore their perspectives and how this impacts on children's play choices. The examples from children's play explain why aspects of play are considered empowering behaviour. The chapter is broken down into three key areas to explain empowering behaviours: children's choices and decisions; the context of play in respect of the environment and resources; and interactions between children.

At the end of the last chapter a definition of empowerment identified three key themes that empower children in play – participation, voice and ownership. This chapter begins to unpack how those key themes can be identified through observing children's social play in unstructured, adult-free situations.

Children's choices and their decisions

In every play interaction, children make choices and decisions about what they want to do and how long they want to do it for. Children make decisions about how they are going to act and also how they are going to react to other children around them. The examples in this section feature Milo and Lucy and show them playing in different social play situations. Their play experiences differentiate the choices and decisions they make and examine how those can be connected, for example it could be argued that children need the skill of determination *and* persistence in order to meet their play challenges. However, what one person considers determination another might judge as recklessness. Therefore some shared definitions are needed as well as an explanation of the choices made to categorise those play behaviours. The following play from the research exemplifies this.

Indicators of empowering play behaviour 45

Motivating play: Milo and the pipe

Milo is outside in the courtyard of the private day nursery he attends. He has picked up a long piece of black pipe. He is walking around with it, sometimes holding it horizontally and sometimes vertically. Another child has picked up a length of wood. These materials are part of the outdoor play experience at the nursery and the boys have seen them and played with them before. Milo goes over to the child with the length of wood. They stand side by side together for a while, then Milo holds out his pipe encouraging the other child to hold his length of wood beside it. Both boys look up. The wood is longer than the pipe and Milo appears to be comparing them (see Figure 4.1). He holds his pipe up in the air as if to try and make the pipe higher than the wood, but the child with the plank of wood does the same, instantly making it much higher. Milo lets the pipe rest on the floor and turns away from the child, walking towards an educator who is engaged with another child. He returns to the other child who is now leaning his plank of wood against a brick wall. Milo follows his lead in placing his pipe next to the wood. Then he starts to move the pipe, reaching it up the wall to try and make it longer than the length of wood. He shows the educator what he is doing when she comes over.

FIGURE 4.1 Milo and his friend comparing lengths

In the video, Milo is showing high levels of interest. This is defined as wanting to be part of something through engaging with an object or other children involved in the same sort of play. Children show their interest in other children's actions and play through their desire to be part of the play or game, their excitement through their body language or verbal communication. Interest can also be shown through modelling the same play in an attempt to join in with established play or through gestures which suggest to other children that they would like to participate.

He is also engaging in challenge although he might not recognise this. He is engrossed in play that an adult may perceive as being risky (walking around with a long pipe) but he is oblivious to any perceived danger and is only concerned with the continuation of the play. Readdick and Park (1998) consider that children in general are explorative and seek out ways in which they can challenge themselves. The physical and social situation that they find themselves in may determine whether their play behaviour is perceived as a risk or a challenge. A situation where children display positive emotions such as a 'have a go' attitude may influence how children approach certain play situations and consequently whether they are challenging themselves or taking a risk.

Milo is using his initiative. He is actively engaged in doing something different from the rest of the other children. Using his initiative Milo has moved away from other children to pursue his own play. Regardless of what other children think or do, he continues with his ideas for a sustained period. Initiative can also be seen by children who by following their own play may take a small number of other children with them, capturing their imagination with the idea. They may also initiate change within the whole group, taking the play in a new direction based on the original idea or initiate a completely new idea that other children want to be a part of.

From the example it is also clear that Milo is also demonstrating persistence. This is when children are engaged in something for the sake of doing it, stimulated by their own interest. They are involved in continuous, extended engagement where they are motivated to take part or explore their own abilities or emotions without being prompted by someone else to do so. They seek out opportunities to pursue their individual interests regardless of what other children are doing. Hughes (2001) refers to the idea of persistence as intrinsic motivation where a child is compelled to play and because of that make choices and decisions over how they play and what they play with.

In Table 4.1 the definitions relating to interest, challenge, initiative and persistence are mapped to the play that Milo engages in.

Overall Milo is demonstrating motivation in his play because he is following his own conviction, choices and interests. He has some support from his peers, but the play is his own idea which he persists with and challenges himself to make his pipe reach higher than the length of wood. The play is directed by Milo and therefore consists of an open-ended process. The motivation to play is driven by him, leading his own play and involving another child in comparing the length of the wood and pipe. Andrews (2012, p. 19) suggests that children are motivated when they

Indicators of empowering play behaviour 47

TABLE 4.1 Coding Milo's play

Focus child		Milo
Location of video clip		City centre private day nursery: outside
Total length of video clip		01.03.28
Codes	**Timing**	**Description**
Interest	00.00.00–00.07.51	Milo compares the length of his pipe with another child's length of wood. They both look up to see which is longer. They turn away from comparing the materials at the same time.
Initiative	00.09.30–00.15.85	Milo lifts his pipe into the air holding just one end of the pipe, making it go higher. The other child follows his actions.
Challenge	00.27.95–00.42.98	Milo watches the other child lean his length of wood against the wall. He follows his actions, but then tries to stretch his pipe higher up the wall by lifting it up. The other boy then tries to do the same.
Persistence	00.53.34–01.03.28	Milo and the other boy keep trying to lift their piece of wood/pipe up the wall to see whose can go higher.

choose how and when to play with the 'impulse to play coming from the child as they seek opportunities to pursue their interests'.

Another of the children, Amy, is also highly motivated in her play. Amy's mother comments on her child's motivation to stay focused on what she is playing with after reviewing some of her daughter's play at home and at nursery:

> She does her own thing most of the time at home, I just let her get on with whatever she is playing and she can concentrate on that for a long time, she doesn't need me to be with her. She is the same at nursery; I sometimes have to drag her away from what she is playing with the other children.

The motivation to play enables children to express their preferences and become powerful social participants in their own right in the way they are able to make choices and decisions. The lead educator from the children's centre reflected on how children's motivation and their decision-making skills impact on opportunities for play:

> There was a little girl playing today that doesn't normally speak, that stands back and doesn't join in, but there was a 'wow' moment today to see her running around with a bucket in hand going 'well I'll get this and I'll put this over here and we'll do this' and actually joining in. And for Mum that was a 'wow' moment as well. We have all noticed that she has made that transition

48 Indicators of empowering play behaviour

to being part of the group rather than standing back and just being on the periphery all the time.

The desire to want to play and be motivated to join in with others for this little girl has opened up a whole range of new opportunities, experiences and potential for engaging and making new friends. As with Milo, they are demonstrating the significance of being motivated through play to make new discoveries.

Empathy

In many of video observations children were empathetic to other children in the same play situation and they showed this in a number of ways through the choices they made in their play and their communication with other children. The children had choices about their responses and behaviour towards other children, and displays of empathy towards each other were an important feature of how they chose to express themselves. Empathy emerged as a recurring sub-theme in all of the play situations, as this next interview extract with Lucy's mother illustrates.

> I saw her once at nursery, a group of them were playing together and it was clear that another little girl was in charge. A little boy was getting really cross, because she wouldn't listen to him and Lucy just went straight up to him and gave him a big hug! She wasn't prompted or anything, just saw that he was upset and she wanted to make it better. I thought that was lovely.

In this next example, Lucy and Emma are fascinated by a wind chime and it is the respectful interaction between the two girls which contributes to the idea of empathy in play.

Empathetic play: Lucy and the wind chime

Lucy and Emma outside at the rural private day nursery they attend. They are under a wooden canopy looking up at a wind chime that has been hung there. Emma stands on an upturned crate to reach for the chime and swings it so that it makes a noise. Lucy asks to have a go but she is shorter than Emma and finds it difficult to reach. She stretches her arm as far as she can and just manages to touch the bottom of the chime. Emma looks around for more crates to stack so it is easier for Lucy to reach. Lucy sees a chair a short distance away and brings that over so she can stand on it to reach the chime more easily (see Figure 4.2).

The girls are both following and listening to each other in the process of the play and also problem-solving in getting the best out of the wind chime by getting a higher chair to stand on so it can be reached more easily. They are turn-taking and both immersed in what they want to do. They are empowered in the play situation, both being able to make the wind chime work and sharing the experience with their friend. Allison et al. (2011) suggest that being able to empathise encourages a connection with

Indicators of empowering play behaviour 49

FIGURE 4.2 Lucy standing on a crate at the rural private day nursery

others, helps to understand others' feelings and behaviour and respond in appropriate ways. In the video sequence the girls are connected to each other in the game they are playing. They understand each other's feelings in terms of wanting to reach the chime and recognising the importance of having an equal chance to do so. They respond sensitively and appropriately to each other through taking turns, helping each other climb up to the wind chime and reading each other's body language, for example when Lucy wobbles on the crate, Emma stretches out her arms to help steady her.

In Table 4.2, the interactions between the children are mapped to the description of the video content. Taken as individual actions they may not seem to be contributing to being empathetic, but as a play episode they illustrate the connection and understanding between the two girls. This can be very powerful in identifying play that is perhaps deemed as unremarkable, yet still empowering.

When a child is willing to share their play resources with another child, they are drawing on their knowledge and understanding of the social or cultural rules and etiquette that they have learned from their parents and through participating in a community of social interactions.

This is not exclusive to children's use of language, or who can shout the loudest, but about the subtle ways in which children use their voice to attract attention from other children, support their peers or change the play situation. Sometimes children use their verbal communication in very deliberate ways with purpose to achieve an

50 Indicators of empowering play behaviour

TABLE 4.2 Coding Lucy and Emma's play

Focus child	Lucy
Location of video clip	Rural private day nursery: outside
Total length of video clip	02.01.30

Codes	Timing	Description
Verbal communication	00.38.78–00.07.10	Lucy asks the other child 'can I have a go?' and Emma lets her.
Following	00.46.44–01.09.21	Lucy is trying to reach the wind chime from the upturned crate, following Emma's turn. She is stretching for the chime and eventually reaches it to swing it so that it makes a sound.
Listening	00.48.88–01.07.10	Lucy is listening to Emma explaining how to reach up to the wind chime and the best way to move it so that it makes a sound. She then copies her actions when it is her turn.
Knowledge	01.30.65–01.55.30	Lucy is trying to reach the wind chime. She keeps trying, but the wind is spinning it, making it difficult to catch. Lucy gets a chair which is higher than the upturned crate, to position under the chime so that she is able to reach the chime once she has stood on it.

end, but in other situations the impact of children's verbal communication can be unexpected to the child who initiated the exchange. It is interesting then to see how verbal communication influences other children, how they respond and how the child who initiated the communication manages the situation.

In the example Lucy demonstrates her knowledge through physical actions indicating implicit understanding in what she is doing. The girls model each other's physical actions, and show understanding of the emotional responses the play facilitates. In this case it is the excitement and a sense of achievement when the wind chime is reached and activated. They also show empathy in understanding how each other is feeling in wanting to play with the chime but not being able to do so without solving the problem of being able to reach it.

Empathy as part of empowerment is challenging to pinpoint and in many of the examples, is very subtle. However, in reviewing the whole of the data that informed the research into empowerment and comparing the children in this book, empathy in children's play is evident and an important aspect of an empowering experience. In many of the examples children show that they are able to understand somebody else's feelings and are sensitive to those feelings in their own play.

The context of children's play: environment and resources

Children's play can support the process of empowerment through different opportunities and experiences and social interactions. Understanding the contribution of the play environment towards the processes of empowerment is important because it influences the way in which children come together and impacts on what they decide to do in that space. Children sometimes use space in ways that are unexpected and highly creative. For example, in Chapter 5, Edward and his friends use branches and trees in the outdoor space, incorporating them into imaginative games where they become creatures with their own personalities. Waller (2006) suggests that opportunities to play in natural environments are valuable and significant to children's experiences and general well-being. Outdoor play in particular is seen to evoke a desire for children to be more physical in their actions, for example wanting to climb trees and being more animated in their verbal responses. Langston and Abbott (2005) discuss how children's play is influenced by their immediate environment as they use the resources available to them to develop and master skills, explore and problem solve, be creative and use their imagination. Therefore environments that encourage play and challenge children enable them to demonstrate initiative and risk taking.

The children in the examples, although potentially influenced by their environment, did not rely on it solely to provide them with play ideas. There was never a moment where the children looked as if they had run out of things to do or asked 'what shall we do now?' There was a desire and motivation to use whatever resources they found within the different play contexts to follow their own interests, ideas and explorations. In terms of empowerment, the range of contexts where children were observed provided opportunities for participation, for children to have a voice through what they said or did and to have a sense of ownership within their play. Consequently, empowerment in play is not determined or restricted by the context, but is influenced by children's actions and reactions within that context and the possibilities available through play. The key worker for Milo in the city centre day nursery explains how she feels the environment supports empowerment: 'Empowerment sounds like a really strong word, but here [at the setting] we let children have free access to whatever they want, follow their interests and give them opportunity to explore them whether that is inside or outside.'

The next example illustrates how children who have freedom in their play utilise the environment to explore different possibilities.

Coordinated play: Jade is in charge!

In the private day nursery in the rural countryside the outdoor space has an extensive undulating grassed area and a group of children gather round a black pipe. The pipe is large enough for a child to crawl through it, which is what staff expected the children to do when they discovered it as a new resource in their outside space. Jade runs up to the pipe and stands to one side of it. She tries to climb over the top and as she does so it rolls away from her. She stops and gives it a push. Again the pipe rolls away from her, this time a little further. She pushes a bit harder, this time running up to it so she has more force behind the push. Other children start to come over, they can see what Jade is doing and want to join in. Jade has an idea. She starts to arrange the children on one side of the pipe, giving instructions of where to stand

and not to touch the pipe until she says so. The children are excited, but follow her orders. When she has them in place she tells them to push and as a joint effort the pipe starts to move (see Figure 4.3). The children keep up with the pipe as it rolls along the ground, picking up speed. They come to a bit of a hill. The pipe starts to slow and Jade realises that they will need to put more effort in to roll it up the bank. She shouts, 'push harder!', which the children do, but it is quite a task. When they stop pushing, the pipe starts to roll back towards them. Jade shouts 'again!' but for some the effort is too great and they move away from the pipe. Jade is left to try and manage the pipe on her own. She steps back as it comes to a halt. Then the other children join her again and some move to the end of the pipe to start to crawl through. They change the game and Jade walks off, not interested in going through the pipe.

Through the video observation Jade is demonstrating that she has skill in coordinating the other children to achieve her aim of rolling the pipe. She is finding it challenging to push it on her own and so by coordinating the other children to help her, she engages them in a common goal and is empowered in her own motivation, but also in the coming together of the other children. Jade has independent thought about what she wants to do in her play. Not only did the children have to coordinate their own decisions about whether to support Jade in her play, they had to synchronise their movements in the play space, and be considerate of the other

FIGURE 4.3 Jade and friends rolling the pipe

Indicators of empowering play behaviour 53

children around them. Their ability to do this allowed them not only to participate in play but also have ownership of their role within the play. Hughes (2001) recognises that children's coordination is significant in their play because it supports them not only to be adaptable in their physical movements but also in their verbal and non-verbal responses to other children through their actions and gestures. The extract below is from Jade's childminder who viewed the video footage of her engaging the other children in rolling the pipe. It offers an interesting perspective of how Jade achieves this kind of coordination:

> She knows what she is doing when she is playing and she is not afraid to let everyone else know as well! I think sometimes the other children think she is a bit bossy; she tells them what to do and how to do it, but somehow she gets them all involved and in the end everyone is playing along with her whether they intended to or not.

In Table 4.3, Jade's coordination highlights how she uses her skill to achieve a sense of empowerment from the play and the significance of the environment and resources in helping her achieve her aim.

The characteristics linked to the overriding idea of children coordinating their actions to achieve a goal within their play are closely linked to children's motivation to play. Hughes (2001) argues that the essence of play is based on children's intrinsic

TABLE 4.3 Coding of Jade's rolling the pipe play

Focus child	Jade
Location of video clip	Private day nursery: outside
Total length of video clip	02.02.32

Codes	Timing	Description
Interest	00.00.00–00.16.79	Jade and other children are standing one side of a large pipe, pushing it with their hands to see what happens. The pipe starts to roll across the field.
Verbal communication	00.17.05–00.22.36	Jade shouts to the other children to keep pushing the pipe.
Non-verbal communication	00.33.21–00.50.45	Jade continues to try and push the pipe even when the other children have given up. Her physical effort indicates that she wants to continue. This encourages other children to re-join her and give rolling the pipe another go.
Interest	00.51.60–01.02.73	Jade looks with the other children into the end of the pipe where a child had crawled but she doesn't crawl inside. She then runs away from the pipe.
Flexible environment	00.15.17–00.27.89	The space in the field allows Jade to run away from the game that the other children are involved in and return as and when she wants to.

desire and curiosity. He believes that play is something that children have to do and can be evidenced through children's interactions with different opportunities and their motivation to use those opportunities to satisfy their curiosity. In the video sequence Jade has a strong desire to roll the pipe and through her motivation to do this and her ability to coordinate the other children she is able to achieve her aim.

Play is a continuum of opportunities where children incorporate the world around them, stimulating qualities such as curiosity, creativity and inventiveness. The process of play can evoke strong emotional responses depending on the play situation and can be a positive and/or negative experience for children. Whalen (1995) maintains that children explore a sense of who they are, especially as they develop relationships with their peers and explore social situations together through play. A play situation may not always be a comfortable space for children as they may feel the need to conform to what their peers are saying or doing, for example they may feel pressured to 'prove' themselves in risk-orientated play. Jade's mother supports this view in her reflection on her daughter's play:

> She is always involved in whatever is going on and likes to be at the centre of it all. She has older siblings so I don't know if it is about trying to keep up with them or prove to herself that she can do all the things they are doing or that desire not to be left out. It certainly means that she is opinionated! And although I can see that her brothers get a bit frustrated that she is always there when they want to do something more physical, like climb trees, they do try to include her and she will give anything a go.

How the environment and resources can support children's imagination

In each play situation children were freely able to use their imagination to develop their play both as individuals and in a group with other children. It was evident that children were sometimes immersed in their own imaginative game, whilst playing alongside others, in parallel play, whereas at other times they shared their imaginative thoughts with other children as a way of encouraging them to play the same game. Imaginative ideas and play were owned by the children and how these were extended, adapted or changed was driven by the play situation and the other children present. The following extract from an interview with Milo's mother corroborates Sawyer's (1997) observation that imagination and creativity in play is perpetuated by the interplay between children especially in social group situations.

> Milo has got a great imagination, he thinks up all sorts of things triggered by perhaps something he has picked up at nursery or something that he has seen on TV. He is able to go, almost into his own world, you know? Lose himself in what he has created in his head and then plays it out with his friends.

Indicators of empowering play behaviour 55

In the next example, Milo demonstrates his imagination through pretending to be a horse show-jumping over obstacles he has constructed in his garden at home.

Imaginative play: Milo the showjumper

Milo is at home in the garden. He appears to be running circuits of the garden, jumping over obstacles in his way such as outdoor chairs, toys lying in the grass, garden tools and flower pots (see Figure 4.4). He is running across the lawn, down the steps, across the patio and up onto the lawn again. He repeats this over and over again, sometimes holding his arms up in front of him as if he were an animal and interchanging between a normal running action and a skipping movement. Towards the end of the video sequence, Milo announces to his mother that he is show-jumping and he has won. His mother gives him a pretend medal, making the action of placing it over his head as they do in the Olympics and he announces he is now going to do the hurdles.

Table 4.4 shows how the characteristics of play are linked to what Milo is doing and how these can be linked to the way in which the environment and resources within it facilitate his imagination.

In their play behaviour children actively search for thrills and excitement to push the boundaries of the physical limits set by the environment they are in. Children may

FIGURE 4.4 Milo demonstrating his show-jumping skills

TABLE 4.4 Coding Milo's imaginative play

Focus child	Milo
Location of video clip	Home
Total length of video clip	02.36.40

Codes	Timing	Description
Challenge	01.50.42–02.06.16	Milo is running circuits of the garden, jumping over things that are in his way. He falls over after coming down the patio steps, but gets back up and carries on. He then falls up the steps but again carries on.
Involving an adult	02.15.59–02.36.44	Milo tells his mother he is show-jumping and he has won. She gives him a medal for his achievement, recreating the podium at the Olympics where he accepts his medal from her.
Flexible resources	00.30.25–00.55.12	Milo uses the natural environment of the garden and his own constructions to create show jumps and invent a course to jump.
Flexible environment	00.35.55–02.35.40	Milo uses the garden as a show-jumping track, adapting his jumping technique to incorporate the different aspects of the garden such as the steps and then using these at the end of the play as the medal podium.
Verbal communication	02.15.59–02.36.44	Milo is able to convey to his mother his reasons for his play as he explains he is show-jumping and what he is planning to do next in winning the hurdles.

be hesitant or look for reassurance from others while involved in risk taking or before engaging in the play. This is not the case with Milo, probably because he is in his home environment which is very familiar to him and the fact that he has choice in how to use the obstacles in his way. If he doesn't feel like jumping over a chair, he can miss it out and justify it as part of his play. Ball et al. (2008) considers that children have an active appetite for risk and will seek out ways in which they can push their boundaries and capabilities. This may happen in a variety of different play situations and involve different play types such as play with objects (Smith, 2005). In Hughes (2006) and the taxonomy of play, risky play may have elements of different types of play such as exploratory play (exploration of the unknown and of new and different ways of playing), locomotor play (intense movement and physically active play), mastery play (testing and challenging own physical abilities and mastery of the environment) as well as the more common play types associated with risk such as rough and tumble play.

Vygotsky (1978) believed that play is socially situated and is highly dependent upon the context of the play environment. In a play situation, children have opportunities to think in more complex ways because of the variety of factors that can be influential and unpredictable. For example, the way in which children use the environment can influence the direction of their play and the use of resources within that environment can be used by children in ways that have just not occurred to adults. Milo's mother was quite perplexed when he started to run round the garden. The context of the play was not clear to her and she was fearful he might hurt himself. As the play progressed the imaginative elements of the play became clearer, the way Milo said, 'giddy up horsey' and 'whoa!' gave an indication that he was involved in a pretend situation. Vygotsky (1966) recognised play as an important tool to support children's intellectual and social development, emphasising the way children's imagination could be linked to developing confidence through practising skills. 'In play the child is always behaving beyond his age, above his usual everyday behaviour: in play he is, as it were, a head above himself' (Vygotsky, 1978, p. 74). He also maintained that one of the benefits of play is that it offers children opportunities to suspend reality and liberate themselves from the immediate constraints of real-life situations; and this opens opportunities for the exploration of pretend characters, events or objects. As Bodrova (2008) points out, when children play they act in accordance with ideas they have generated and are motivated to explore through their play rather than consciously applying reality. For instance, when children are engaged in symbolic play, they might use an object for a purpose different to its original function, for example using a hairbrush to symbolise a microphone. Children play within real-world constructions, for example, understanding the functions of a microphone, but use pretend situations to develop their play. Children's ability to suspend reality when they are engaged in play and to sustain that suspension for the duration of the play supports Vygotsky's contention that the significance of imagination and cognition is realised where reality, creativity and imagination coincide.

Interactions between children

Children's play experiences and the familiarity of their immediate context supports their self-confidence in the play space and their interaction with other children around them. In the research, children demonstrated their cultural understanding through their play: this revealed what they knew about initiating and sustaining social relationships as well as their understanding of boundaries and what they could and could not do within a particular context. For example, in all of the settings, the children knew the boundaries of what was acceptable, what they could do within the space and how far they could venture before being told by an adult to come back. The children who attended more than one setting knew what was acceptable at the different locations and adapted their play accordingly. They recognised that they could engage with more physical play in the forest school, moving logs and branches where they wanted and that there were different rules and expectations of them when in a more structured environment such as a day nursery. Robinson and Jones Diaz (2006, p. 5) suggest that this is because children are capable of engaging with issues of different rules and ways of doing things, accepting different cultures, and that they 'actively regulate not only their own behaviour, but also that of others around them'. The flexibility and diversity offered by all of the settings enabled

58 Indicators of empowering play behaviour

children to have a sense of control within their play space which supported them to develop a sense of ownership over what they were doing.

In the next example, Michael is playing with Tom in a childminder's setting. It highlights the negotiation between the two boys who both want to play with the same toy car. Their problem-solving skills ensure that on a practical level the play can continue without an argument or falling out.

Problem-solving in play: making a wind-up car work

Michael and Tom are selecting toy cars from a large plastic container (see Figure 4.5). Michael is selecting the cars he wants to play with and lining them up beside him. He finds a car that works with a wind-up key that is supposed to speed across the floor when released. Michael is trying to make it work but the mechanism is being temperamental. Tom is interested in what Michael is doing and is eager to take the car from him and see if he can make it work. Michael is reluctant to hand it to his friend and Tom becomes more vocal in suggesting ways to make it work. He stands over Michael reaching down to try and take the car, but Michael pulls it closer to him so Tom can't take it. He tries harder to release the mechanism as he does not want to relinquish the toy. There is some heated discussion between the boys about why it is not working. Tom realises that he is not going to have the chance to try and make the car work himself so makes some practical suggestions of what Michael could try. Michael, having no further ideas himself, follows Tom's instructions to see if they work to make the car speed across the floor.

FIGURE 4.5 Michael and Tom with the toy cars

Problem-solving is evident in many of the play episodes observed during the research when children could be seen to be participating with other children concerned with the same problem, and when children communicated with each other to articulate their ideas. The need to engage in problem-solving brought children together in many situations. As the extract below from the interview with Michael's mother indicates, children's engagement in problem-solving, exchanging ideas and developing ways of working together often result in creative responses, which Loveless (2009) considers an integral part of the process of play.

> He's a bit of a thinker. He will sit there and work it out, it doesn't matter how long it will take and he gets a bit cross if another child suggests something he has already tried or thought about ... He'll join in though if something is going on, like one of his friends got stuck in the branches of the tree at the nursery and he helped him get down; work out where to step and where to hold onto until he was down.

Table 4.5 shows how Michael's knowledge and instruction enables him to be empowered in the situation because he is able to keep the toy car and stay in control of the situation. He is working with Tom, but does not want to give up the overall responsibility of making the car work. He uses his skills in negotiation and instruction to stay in control.

TABLE 4.5 Coding Michael's problem-solving play

Focus child	Michael
Location of video clip	Childminder
Total length of video clip	02.01.36

Codes	Timing	Description
Knowledge	00.16.36–00.40.02	Michael knows how the car works with the key to make it travel across the floor. He shows Tom how it works, but the mechanism is being temperamental. Michael knows the car won't work on the carpet, but needs a wooden floor to go fast.
Verbal communication	00.16.36–00.40.02	Michael explains to the other child how the car works with the key so that it will travel across a hard floor.
Instruction	01.24.67–01.39.39	He says 'I just want to do this one and you can do the other one', giving instruction to Tom.
Negotiation	01.40.20–01.55.36	Tom wants to have the car to see if he can make it work, but Michael holds on to it, saying 'I can make it work, just hold on'. He is struggling to take the key out of the car to see if he can make it work but is reluctant to give the car to Tom. He says, 'I just have an idea, give me a minute, let me see if this works'. This delays handing over the toy to Tom. He goes on, 'when I have tried this, you can have it and see if it works on the smooth floor'.

In this example, the interaction between the children is central to solving the problem of making the toy car work. Michael is in control of the negotiations because he has got the car in his possession and uses his skills of negotiation; not wanting to relinquish it to Tom and not wanting to have an argument with him. Michael attempts to show he is willing to compromise but tries to persuade Tom that his idea and way of trying to make the car work will be successful. He puts his point of view across verbally and through showing Tom his idea with the resources available to him. Michael also uses instruction to help manage the situation and to stay in possession of the car. He knows that the car will only work properly on a hard surface and pacifies Tom with this knowledge and the promise that he will let Tom have the first go once the car is fixed. Michael presents this as 'rules' of the game and what they can and cannot do in the play space. The rules are an iteration of what an adult has previously told Michael, but they can also be something that the children have devised themselves. Children may invent rules to gain power over other children, convincing them that their way of doing something is correct.

Building a framework of empowerment

Three super-themes of participation, voice and ownership emerged as a result of systematic content analysis through the process of coding the video data in the research. The super-themes were then cross checked with and corroborated by the content analysis of the interview data which gave an overview of the opinions and perspectives of those most closely associated with the children in the study, their parents and educators. The three super-themes were not always transparent in the individual children's play as you may notice from the examples in this chapter. But considering the video sequences overall, together with the interview responses from parents and educators, the themes emerged as recurring and although subtle they were part of supporting children's processes of empowerment.

The super-themes represent the observed commonalities in children's actions and behaviours from the video data across different contexts and provide a basis for rich description of the video and interview analysis (Bernard and Ryan, 2010). As such, children's participation, voice and ownership were discernible in all of the video data and interpretable in the interview data that supports the research.

Figure 4.6 positions the super-themes as interdependent and with the potential to all be present in child-initiated, social play simultaneously or for just one or two to be present. It is apparent that although it does not matter if one, two or all of the super-themes are identifiable in children's play, at least one is needed for a child to be viewed as having an empowering experience. In the clearest examples of children's empowerment, all three super-themes are present during play and parents and educators allude to the themes through their reflections. The sub-themes of motivation, coordination, imagination, problem-solving and empathy categorise recurring instances and actions in children's play which support the development of the super-themes.

Indicators of empowering play behaviour 61

FIGURE 4.6 The empowerment framework: video data codes (in italics) and their relationship to the super-themes (in bold) and sub-themes (underlined) of the research

The relationship is also shown between the systematic coding of children's actions and reactions, capturing instances during the video sequences of children's choices and their decisions, the context of children's play in respect of the environment and resources and interactions between children.

Summary

From the examples of the video sequences in this chapter and from the empowerment framework (Figure 4.6) it is clear that there is potential for overlap and interpretation. For example, the nature of the sub-theme coordination means that it is located between the super-themes of participation and ownership, implying that it is hard not to be actively participating whilst having ownership in play. In the same way, the sub-theme of imagination is located between the super-themes of ownership and voice but is also open to interpretation depending upon the play situation and how children respond to what is happening and how the play develops. Problem-solving perhaps aligns more closely with the super-theme of participation if the codes alone were taken into account, but in the example of Michael and Tom playing with the toy car, Michael is asserting his voice and controlling what is happening in the play through his knowledge of the car and how it works.

The next chapter considers what participation, voice and ownership, the three super-themes needed for empowerment in play, look like in practice.

5

EXPLORING CHILDREN'S PARTICIPATION, VOICE AND OWNERSHIP THROUGH PLAY

This chapter analyses the three main (super) themes that inform the book. Organised into three sub-sections, participation, voice and ownership, are discussed in relation to children's empowerment in play and how each theme is interrelated. These themes enable a picture of empowerment to emerge, identifying the processes involved for individual children, exemplified through play examples including:

- Edward den making with his peers outside at the children's centre, providing a rich example of participation between children;
- Harry involved in imaginative play with his friend at the city centre private day nursery, giving an example of how he uses his voice within the play situation;
- Michael concentrating on climbing car tyres to slide down a pole outside at the rural private day nursery, illustrating his sense of ownership over his play.

The analysis of these three examples is also supported by extracts from the reflections from parents and educators. Each example contains a synopsis of the video that gives an overview of what happened in the whole of the sequence followed by a breakdown of how the sequence was coded, including the video timing. The sub-themes outlined in Chapter 4 are applied to the examples, indicating the relationship between the coding applied to all of the video data and the overall themes of the research identifying indicators of empowerment.

Participation

Research suggests that children's participation in play is significant to the process of empowerment because the nature of their participation shapes and directs what is happening and can potentially change or develop children's interests or build capacity for ongoing play (Hart, 1997). Thomas (2007) argues that participation can mean being listened to or just being present when a major decision-making event occurs. Active participation, however, is more significant and means being involved, by investing in social interactions with others and risking an emotional investment in caring about what is going on and wanting to be part of that situation (Else, 2014). Active participation could also be taken to imply empowerment of those involved in the sense 'that children believe and have reason to believe that their involvement will make a difference' (Sinclair, 2004, p. 111). Participation is more than expressing individual choice, as it is part of a broader experience of belonging and feeling valued (Bae, 2009). Thus, children may become powerful social participants in their own right as play allows them to express their preferences and interests. Where these are accepted by other children, this signals that their views are important (Else, 2014). Participation, therefore, has a wider meaning, it is not just about actively participating with peers, it is also about children being able to make choices and decisions, about having the opportunity to be curious and explore, and to feel that they are included and wanted as part of the play. In its widest sense, this involves a process of empowerment because the motivation for play is child-initiated and subsequently sustained for as long as children's interests remain active.

The following example considers participation specifically within the context of children's play and is analysed as a process involving the social relationships taking place between children's peer social relationships rather than between adults and children. Participation emerges as an overriding theme because, for all of the children in the study, the video analysis of their play revealed that they had choices: they could make the decision to start or join an existing play situation; if they wanted to, they could make a connection and participate with another child or group of children. Once play was underway, there was then a constant underlying process of negotiation among children as to whether to simply be involved or to lead the play; whether to contribute through words or actions; how to position themselves alongside other children who they felt comfortable with; whether to argue their point and/or consider whether their view was worth fighting for.

The data indicates that as well as choosing whether or not to join an existing play situation, participation also involves children making active decisions about the level of social investment they want to make; that is what they chose to do and how they chose to behave and react towards other children. Thus, their contribution in play is through their actions and active engagement with other children and, as Treseder (1997) suggests, can be seen to reflect the cultural context in which they are situated. In terms of the settings observed here, all of the social play situations offer opportunities for participation between children without adult intervention, and this enables children to take part on their own terms.

The example below shows Edward and his two friends as they look for sticks and branches to build their den in the woodland area of the city centre children's centre forest school. Table 5.1 is a written account of the video sequence, the coding decisions made and how those codes correspond to the sub-themes of empowerment.

Participation in den making: Edward and his 'Ben 10' treehouse

Edward is playing with three other boys, outside in the woodland area. He is collecting large sticks and leaning them against a tree to make a 'Ben 10' treehouse (Ben 10 is a cartoon character, on television, who has a watch-like alien device that allows him or anyone who wears it to turn into alien creatures). The other boys are joining in the play, adding sticks to the pile. Edward collects sticks from nearby and brings them back to build the den. He is talking to the other children, suggesting what they could do next and what he wants to do (see Figure 5.1). Some of the other boys protest at his actions and suggestions, but Edward carries on and moves onto collecting more sticks quickly, largely ignoring what the others are saying.

This video sequence illustrates the features identified earlier in relation to the super-theme of participation in a number of ways. The focus is on Edward who is at the centre of the play and instructing others and taking the lead. Some of the other children have a different agenda to Edward about what they want to do with the sticks: Edward, however, is able to motivate the group to stay on-task and support what he intends to do. He is able to be adaptable and develop the play so that the den eventually becomes a 'Ben 10' treehouse. Edward leads the process of play, including the children that want to join in, negotiating with the other children over the resources and building of the den. He is actively participating, physically building the den and believes that his contribution is making a difference within the play space. Edward has his own agenda in the play, but he realises he cannot build the den without the help of the other children and therefore has to balance his motivation to finish the den with

FIGURE 5.1 Edward taking the lead in den making

TABLE 5.1 Coding participation

Focus child		Edward
Location of video clip		Children's centre: outside
Total length of video clip		02.06.11

Codes	Timing	Description
Verbal communication Links to sub-theme: coordination	00.06.23– 00.10.90	Edward verbally encourages the children to build a 'Ben 10' treehouse. He describes the sticks as 'big and fat' and tries to organise the other children in bringing sticks to build the structure of the den.
Knowledge Links to sub-theme: problem-solving	00.05.12–00.12.01	Edward knows what to do with the sticks in order to build a den against a large tree. He uses the tree as the main support for the sticks so that the den structure can start to take shape.
Negotiation Links to sub-theme: coordination	00.50.14–00.58.20	Edward negotiates with another boy over a large stick and persuades him to let go of the stick so he can place it where he wants it.
Instruction Links to sub-theme: problem-solving	01.00.01–01.04.55	Edward tells another child what to do with a stick in order to help build the den. He tells some other boys to stop playing in the mud and come and help.
Determination Links to sub-theme: motivation/problem- solving	01.08.08–01.15.22	Edward along with another boy moves a long, twisted stick into position. They have several attempts, lifting the stick above their heads to lean it against the tree trunk.
Sharing Links to sub-theme: coordination	01.09.68–01.13.74	Edward shares the task of moving the long, twisted stick into position. The boys are working together to place it where they want it.
Interest Links to sub-theme: motivation/imagination	01.19.41–01.20.95	Edward shows interest in keeping a narrative going alongside building the den by suggesting that they go to bed, using his imagination to maintain a story.
Instruction Links to sub-theme: motivation	01.30.11–01.34.16	Edward shouts to someone out of shot 'Hey come over here, this is our "Ben 10" treehouse'.
Determination Links to sub-theme: motivation	02.00.21–02.06.52	Edward is on his own, as the other children have moved away from the play. He picks up a large stick and declares 'I'm taking this'.

the realisation that other children also want to contribute. The educator who reviewed the video commented:

> Edward was there at the forefront of it, but I thought they all worked really well together. They were all still contributing and going slightly further afield to look, you know, once they had got the sticks and logs that were close to the den, they knew to extend that search so that was lovely as well ... There was a lot of reinforcement between them, if Edward said something; others would reinforce it by repeating it.

The analysis of 'den making' also illustrates how Edward's actions and behaviours can be described in terms of three sub-themes, motivation, coordination and problem-solving, that together contribute to the super-theme of participation. In the empowerment framework 'determination' is positioned between two sub-themes, motivation and problem-solving. In this example, Edward's determination to move a large stick and place it to become part of the den structure indicates his intentions that he is not going to give up on moving the stick; that he knows exactly where he wants to place it and is going to make it happen. He has help, but is the driving force behind ensuring that the stick finds its place within the den. He is problem-solving as he goes along, trying to lift and twist the stick, manoeuvring it into place and instructing the other children as he does this. In leading the play, Edward takes on a coordinating role using his verbal communication to give instruction and to some extent negotiating with the other children. He seamlessly demonstrates his motivation to want to be at the centre of the play, leading what is going on, coordinating their ideas into his own and problem-solving as he goes.

Voice

The interpretation of children's play and their voice within that play centres on their decision-making and how they communicate their decisions to the other children. Moyles (2005) argues that through play children have opportunities to learn from each other and deal with others' expectations and feelings however these are articulated. For example, they learn to express their views not only through speaking but through their actions, body language, gestures or where they position themselves within a group of children (Clark and Moss, 2011). In child-initiated, social play children have a choice in what they do as well as what they choose not to do which demonstrates to other children their preferences and how strongly they feel about them (Pramling Samuelsson and Fleer, 2008). As McCarry (2012) argues, children also have to manage other children's responses not only to their verbal communication, but their actions and consequences of their actions. Here 'children's voice' is taken to refer to how children choose to express themselves in the widest sense and the impact this has on other children playing the same game or in the same space.

Children's spoken voice does not always reflect the reality of their experiences; for example what children say is not always the whole story of what they want or need (Percy Smith, 2006). Children's voice is usually examined within the context of adult–child relationships and Shier (2001) argues that their participation can be expressed in terms of the different levels of involvement that can take place between adults and children. But children's voice is also relevant in child–child relationships and particularly in play situations where children may demonstrate different social and emotional skills in using their voice effectively. Therefore Shier's levels of participation between adults and children may also be applied to child–child relationships in that children in play often:

- listen to the ideas of other children;
- support other children around them in expressing their views through words or actions;
- have their views taken into account by the children around them resulting in action or rejection;
- are actively involved in decision-making;
- take responsibility or the lead in a play situation.

There is interconnectedness between children's voice and participation in child–child relationships in play, as the more children want to be involved, the more opinions they have about the direction of their play. Pramling Samuelsson and Johansson (2006) argue that in order to be creative in play situations, children have to communicate effectively. This means their play is able to evolve, be negotiated and contain a certain amount of compromise so that everyone involved in the play achieves a sense of satisfaction. Children quickly learn through play that if their participation is too dominant or if they attempt to force their views on others, they are often left playing alone; the other children vote with their feet and leave the play space (Hughes, 2001). Children's participation and voice may be closely associated with the process of empowerment as part of experiencing and building social relationships, being involved in play, having ideas affirmed or ignored, and building capacity to be adaptable and flexible in any play situation (Guilbaud, 2003).

In this next example, Harry expresses his play preferences through his game with a friend. At first it seems as if nothing is happening in the play, a non-event without a clear start or finish, but Harry's voice is important in this sequence in determining what happens in the play, what is important to Harry and what he wants to say and do. The complex nature of Harry's voice is integral to empowerment as for him, experiencing and building social connections is not such as straightforward process as it is for Edward. But in this example, Harry is able to be at the centre of the play process, demonstrating his capacity to adapt, and to acknowledge that some of his ideas will be accepted by other children and some will be rejected along the way (see Table 5.2).

Having a voice in play: Harry and a loudspeaker

Harry has a toy loudspeaker; he holds it over his head and accidentally hits his head with the toy. This seems to lead to an idea for a game with his friend

TABLE 5.2 Coding voice

Focus child	Harry
Location of video clip	City centre private day nursery: inside
Total length of video clip	02.03.32

Codes	Timing	Description
Attracting attention Links to sub-theme: imagination	00.22.70–00.36.58	Harry attracts the attention of Joseph by saying 'I'm dead' and pretending to be dead or asleep in a chair.
Interest Links to sub-theme: coordination	00.56.80–01.18.46	Harry shows interest in Joseph developing the play by going along with the rubber ring being placed on his head.
Flexible resources Links to sub-theme: problem-solving/ imagination	00.58.30–01.02.55	The ring and loudspeaker are used to support the boys' exploration of being dead and/or asleep rather than their intended use as a rubber ring and plastic toy.
Verbal communication Links to sub-theme: coordination	01.34.84–01.59.74	Harry and Joseph talk about what they are doing as they play. (This is a particularly important point because of his parents' concern about Harry's speech.)
Listening Links to sub-theme: empathy	01.38.02–01.45.16	Harry listens to Joseph's explanation for the introduction of the rubber ring into the play and accepts it as part of the game. He is connecting with Joseph in going along with what he wants to do.
Negotiation Links to sub-theme: coordination	01.34.84–01.59.74	There is some negotiation between Harry and Joseph in what they will do next and how they are going to use the rubber ring and loudspeaker in their game.
Following Links to sub-theme: empathy	01.33.45–01.59.88	Harry follows Joseph around when he has the loudspeaker, then encourages him to follow when Harry has the rubber ring. Again, his actions support the development of a connection with Joseph.

Joseph. He holds his head and leans over a chair. He then sits in the chair and says to Joseph 'I'm dead'. Joseph takes the loudspeaker from him. Harry ignores him and pretends to be asleep or dead (see Figure 5.2). Joseph uses the loudspeaker in Harry's face. Harry tries not to react. Joseph goes to the shelf and gets a rubber ring and places it on Harry's head. Harry checks what it is with his hand then opens his eyes, looking for Joseph who is hiding behind the chair. Harry gets up and walks away rubbing his head. Joseph follows and they both return to the chair. Joseph sits down and Harry puts a rubber ring on his head. Harry then hides behind the chair. Harry takes the loudspeaker from Joseph who is pretending to be asleep or dead in the chair.

Participation, voice and ownership **69**

FIGURE 5.2 Harry playing dead

The sequence reveals subtle insights into Harry's play and how he expresses himself and uses his imagination. He uses the play resources to keep the interest of Joseph through positioning himself on and behind the chair and using the loudspeaker and rubber ring to support what he wants to do. As the play continues he is aware of how his actions trigger a reaction from his friend and then uses that reaction to continue and adapt the play. Harry uses different ways to communicate with Joseph; verbally but also through what he does and how he uses the environment around him. His mother commented when she reviewed the video sequence:

> Harry didn't talk very much when he was younger and I was quite worried, we went to a speech therapist and that has helped him in his confidence to talk to adults and other children. It's nice to see him sort of in charge here, not so much by what he is saying, but also by how he is reacting to his friend.

The interaction between Harry and his friend in the sequence supports Shier's (2001) view of participation and voice, where children support each other in expressing their views through words or actions. Harry's use of the resources enables him to maintain the interest of the other child as well as express what he wants to do. This also allows Harry to take responsibility and the lead in the play when he attracts Joseph's interest initially, by pretending to be dead. Through his actions he is able to connect with Joseph and adapt his play to ensure that his own interests and exploration of the resources are met, for example, when he copies Joseph's use of the rubber ring. The lead educator from the private day nursery provided an insight into how Harry conveyed the super-theme of voice in this sequence:

> Harry's language sometimes goes into that baby kind of talk, but I think he uses that to his advantage because he can relate to other children easily. He is sophisticated in the way he gets other children to join in and do what he wants without being loud or assertive. At one point he walks off and the other boy actually comes running after him to drag him back into the game again. That says to me that he is an important part of what is going on and knows he doesn't have to shout to be at the centre of what is going on.

The analysis of the video sequence illustrates how Harry's actions and behaviours can be described in terms of two sub-themes, empathy and imagination, that together contribute to the super-theme of voice. The codes of 'listening' and 'following' are positioned in the sub-theme of empathy. In this example, Harry's ability to listen to his friend and follow his ideas allows the play to continue and develop. Harry works with Joseph with a mutual understanding that they both need to be involved and have a say for the game to work and continue. The play has elements of imagination, for example with the theme of being dead which is returned to at different intervals during the play and with each boy taking it in turns to pretend to be dead and/or asleep. This also demonstrates the sub-theme of coordination as throughout the boys are coordinating their actions to continue the play and to problem-solve. For example, Harry wants to get the loudspeaker back and he does this by going along with Joseph's play until he has the opportunity to have the loudspeaker and then creates ways of keeping hold of it. This video sequence is central to the super-theme of voice because, as the lead educator at the children's centre comments:

> It is not always practical to go with what a child wants or it is not always safe to do that, but I think it is important to go with it and see what happens, acknowledging what children have said is really important, but to watch them and see how they express themselves gives me a much better idea of what they want, what they are confident in and what further opportunities I need to plan to give them more confidence.

Harry in his play is able to express his voice through what he is doing and how he is interacting in his play, subtly listening and following his friend, showing empathy and interest in what is happening without having to be loud or opinionated and without dominating other children or resources. He also displays the ability to have ownership over his play, showing a sense of being comfortable in the situation and engaging in active interest with what is going on. The next example is a different play situation, but demonstrates the super-theme of ownership for Michael who is immersed in play involving climbing tyres and sliding down a pole.

Ownership

Children's active interest and engagement in contributing and influencing what is happening and taking a leading role in play provides a basis for owning and developing their play. A sense of ownership can be powerful because children feel confident and safe in the play situation (Robson, 2010; Christensen, 2004). They have knowledge about what might happen and are familiar with other children around them. Ownership supports active interest and engagement in contributing and influencing what happens and taking a leading role in the development of play. Sinclair (2004) contends that recognising children have a vested interest in their play environment also supports the validity of their play agenda, allowing children to follow their own interests and come to their own conclusions.

Through the ownership of play, common interests emerge in the interactions between children; they begin to seek out each other to play with and often the same themes appear. When children cooperate, working towards the same goal or purpose, their play supports a sense that they are in control of the immediacy of their play environment. Ownership also reaffirms familiarity in the processes of common practices which often reflect children's particular community and culture (Christensen, 2004). When there is a sense of ownership in children's play Treseder (1997) argues there may also be characteristics of group cohesiveness in working together, coming up with creative solutions to problems and children feeling able to express their personality and emotions. According to Whalen (1995), ownership in play relates closely to children's knowledge and how they use that knowledge to support the development of their play and involve others.

Ownership in play does not have to be the physical ownership of an object, but can also be ownership of an emotion or memory. Children might share a smile between them, remembering when they last played the same game, or express themselves through their movement; jumping up and down on the spot together in the knowledge that another child is sharing the same feeling. Common interests in play also mean that when the same themes appear children gravitate towards replaying the same game and re-enacting scenarios over and over again. For example, 'Ben 10' was high on the agenda of Edward's play featuring in different contexts but mainly with a group of other boys also obsessed with the television characters. This reflection from the lead educator at the children's centre encapsulates the way in which children's ownership of their play can evolve and how the significance of ownership is realised by educators and parents:

> I have said to some parents, 'why don't you give that a try, or when you go for a walk just ...' and one parent said 'we go for a walk in the fields all the time', but the other day she said, 'we didn't walk, we stopped and did what he wanted to do and that was because of forest school, because we did forest school and I didn't realise that he wanted to do all of these things'. That was maybe investigating the insects or making a den or just standing still and looking at things, and she said, 'that was a real eye opener for me, we used to

go for this walk and I used to think I was providing this wonderful experience for him, but actually I wasn't doing what he wanted to do, I was doing what I thought he wanted to do. When we go now, we don't go as far, we don't need to go as far and we just go at his pace'. For me that is empowerment, for the child to be able to own that experience and be able to get that across to his parent.

The next example of ownership shows Michael just about to attempt to jump onto a pole in order to slide down it, outside at the rural private day nursery. This example illustrates how, by contributing and influencing what is happening and taking a leading role in the development of play, children demonstrate ownership (see Table 5.3).

Ownership in conquering the tyres and pole: Michael's physical play

There are a number of old car tyres stacked near a metal goal post structure outside in the field at the back of the day nursery. Michael and Tom are using the tyres to climb upon, reaching for the upright pole of the goal post and then

TABLE 5.3 Coding ownership

Focus child	Michael
Location of video clip	Private day nursery: outside
Total length of video clip	01.59.00

Codes	Timing	Description
Flexible resources Links to sub-theme: problem-solving	01.25.89–01.42.66	Michael and Tom are stacking four car tyres, making the pile higher, then taking a tyre away and making the stack smaller. Michael holds a tyre upright and moves it towards the metal post and then positions it closer to the stack of tyres for Tom to attempt to stand on the upright tyre.
Initiative Links to sub-theme: motivation	00.36.40–00.50.00	Tom moves away and Michael attempts to climb the stack of tyres alone. He returns and holds the upright tyre steady so Michael can climb up it.
Negotiation Links to sub-theme: coordination	00.20.60–00.29.69	Michael and Tom discuss where the upright tyre should be held so it can be made steady in preparation to be stood on.
Supporting role Links to sub-theme: coordination/problem-solving	01.01.60–01.13.90	Michael holds the upright tyre and the stack for the girl to attempt climbing.
	01.40.57–01.46.80	Michael holds the upright tyre steady with the girl whilst Tom attempts to jump from the tyres to the metal pole.

FIGURE 5.3 Michael making a leap for the pole

attempting to slide down the pole. They first start to stack the tyres, but they are quite heavy and the boys work together to move them closer to the upright goal post and then to stack them one on top of the other. They do not get them perfectly lined up so when Michael attempts to climb onto them, they move and slip out of place. Tom goes around the other side to help steady the tyre stack so Michael can climb up higher. Satisfied that he is as high as he can go, Michael jumps from the tyre stack to grab the pole (see Figure 5.3). He wraps his legs around it, hangs there for a second, before sliding down to the ground. Tom wants to have a go at the same thing, but Michael also wants to have a second turn. As the boys are involved in this discussion, a girl who has been watching the play comes closer. She asks if she can have a turn. The boys look uncertain and try to ignore her, but she asks again. Michael steps aside and the girl attempts to climb the tyres. She is much smaller than the boys and finds it difficult. She has a few attempts before Michael comes back to the tyres and starts to climb them at the same time as the girl. The tyres wobble and the girl backs away from the stack. Michael continues to climb and has another go at sliding down the pole. Tom is quick to start climbing as Michael reaches for the pole so that he gets a turn.

In this video sequence Michael appears confident and comfortable in what he is doing, and his actions fit many of the features of play identified with ownership. He had knowledge of what it takes to get to the top of the pole in order to slide down it and is not afraid to take charge of the situation so he can fulfil what he wants to do. He is actively interested and engaged in the play, influencing what is happening through organising the tyres on the ground. Michael follows his own interests in the pursuit of being able to slide down the pole and has total ownership of the situation, leading and organising the other children. Michael has the support of Tom and the girl who want to do the same thing as he is attempting, but he has control of the immediate environment, something that Treseder (1997) considers important in establishing ownership over a particular space or area. Michael demonstrates his knowledge of the situation and what it takes to achieve his aim of sliding down the pole. He then uses that knowledge to support Tom. Both his mother and the lead educator who reviewed the video commented on this: 'They were empowered from each other. I think it is trust in each other and it was really interesting to see when the little girl went in, the play didn't stop, they just accepted her' (Michael's mother). 'It was their play wasn't it? Michael was totally engrossed in what he was doing. He had a goal and was going to achieve it' (lead educator, rural private day nursery).

In this example of ownership, there are also rich examples of the sub-themes motivation, problem-solving and coordination. Michael seems to be motivated by the challenge of the situation and he demonstrates his complete ownership over the play space in organising the other children, ensuring that he has the best opportunities to climb the tyres and show his skill in sliding down the pole.

In many of the examples of the video data, and especially this one, sometimes the fit between the super-themes and sub-themes are not clear cut and there are elements of overlapping of codes, sub-themes and super-themes. The diagram in Chapter 4 (Figure 4.6) illustrates to some extent the overlap between the themes and as this example demonstrates the codes and sub-themes cannot necessarily be uniquely associated with any one super-theme. The next chapter analyses the implications for this in greater detail.

Summary

This chapter has identified the three super themes to look for in play situations to determine if children are engaging in a process of empowerment. In looking for these, focus is taken away from the outcomes of play and is more interested in what is happening, how children are negotiating their play between them and how they come up with solutions to make the play happen in a way that is acceptable to everyone involved. The skill that Edward, Harry and Michael have in getting what they want out of their play is sophisticated and could be easily overlooked as a non-event, something that the children are doing before something more important happens. But these short episodes of play demonstrate the rich detail available in intimate social processes that enables children to learn and develop their skills in participating, having a voice and owning their play interactions.

6
OBSERVING EMPOWERMENT IN PLAY

This chapter demonstrates how educators can observe empowerment in play through three different examples. It offers practical prompts and questions based on the empowerment framework introduced in Chapter 4 (Figure 4.6) that can be used to develop observations of empowerment in children's play. It is important to consider the meanings that emerge from children's experiences and different perspectives on play. Through direct observation of children's actions and interactions with other children and taking into consideration the situational context and resources, a picture of empowering experiences can emerge.

The chapter highlights how the context of children's play is interwoven with understanding about their daily lives and cultures, observing their interactions and listening to them. Observations need to be flexible, led by children's play choices and fitting in with the early childhood setting's daily routine. A questioning approach provides a platform for exploring children's social worlds, the realities of their play and how they make and sustain connections with other children. This chapter shows how children's individual and group actions and decisions build an account of their social play and how that contributes to empowerment.

Figures 6.1 and 6.2 illustrate the transformation of the empowerment framework to a practical resource for observing play. The empowerment framework maps the super-themes and sub-themes that are important for empowering experiences. However, to avoid the framework becoming a subjective 'tick list' of what children appear to be doing in their play a series of questions prompt educators to really consider what is happening; to put themselves in the children's position and provide a detailed narrative of their play.

The visual representation of the prompt questions illustrates the crossover between sub-themes of motivation, coordination, problem-solving, imagination and empathy into the areas of the super-themes participation, voice and ownership. In practical terms a list of these questions may be more manageable for educators (see

FIGURE 6.1 The empowerment framework

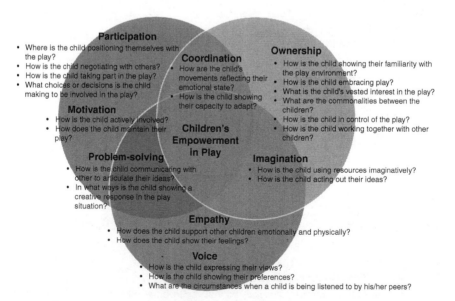

FIGURE 6.2 Empowerment framework with prompt questions to guide educator observations

Table 6.1), although the intersect between the sub- and super-themes is important as it is a visual reminder of the layered nature of empowering experiences.

In table format it is also possible to add the behavioural indicators of empowerment (outlined in Chapter 4) which supports educators in making decisions about how to think and describe what is happening in the play.

A common practice in England is to observe children in planned activities and look for indicators that suggest children's learning and development. Activities are planned around key areas of learning set out in the curriculum and observations and assessment of children's competence then informs further planning. This process has become entrenched in early childhood daily practice (Howard, 2010). The empowerment framework moves away from this so that the indicators of empowerment are contextualised and provide a rich description of experiences that inform learning and development.

The empowerment framework was trialled in two settings as a way of observing children's play. In this first example the educator films Michael. She is his key worker and is building a profile of his empowering experiences. The footage is approximately two minutes long and she analyses the video soon after the children have moved inside and are engaged in a structured activity led by another colleague. The ability to re-watch Michael's play, record his actions and reactions based on the empowerment question prompts to reflect on his play also supports her professional development and understanding of the significance of play. It is quite an undertaking to incorporate the whole of the empowerment framework in one single observation. Therefore in this example the focus is on ownership as the super-theme and coordination as the sub-theme.

Ownership and coordination: Michael's stick fight

Michael is outside in the field area walking around the perimeter which has longer grass. He sees something in the undergrowth and moves closer to investigate. He bends down and pulls out of the long grass a stick which is fairly straight and about a meter in length. He is very happy with what he has found as he grins and does a little hop once he realises how long it is. He looks around, there is no one close by so he begins to drag the stick behind him, moving towards two other boys that are playing in the middle of the field. As the boys see him approach they turn towards him and also see the stick. They immediately move towards it, wanting to touch it. Michael has hold of the one end, and the boys grab the other. The stick is now lifted off the ground and held between the boys. Michael is not very happy about this and lets out a high-pitched cry as he keeps hold of the stick but starts to run.

Taking the others by surprise, they let go as Michael sets off across the field, stick in tow. They run after him and soon catch up. They take the other end of the stick again and start to pull. Michael pulls back and starts to tell them off, 'It's my stick! Let go!' The boys don't let go but Michael turns so his back is against the stick which makes the direction of the stick change to a sideways motion. This takes the other boys by surprise and the force at which Michael does this means that the boys stumble, the stick drops to the ground and the weight of Michael's back makes it snap in two (see Figure 6.3). Michael is left holding one end and the boys the other.

78 Observing empowerment in play

TABLE 6.1 Empowerment framework prompt questions in a grid

Super themes

Participation	Ownership	Voice
• Where is the child positioning themselves within the play? • How are they negotiating with others? • How are they taking part? • What choices and decisions are they making to be involved in the play?	• How is the child showing their familiarity with the play environment? • How are they embracing play? • What are their vested interests in the play? • What are the commonalities between the children? • How are they in control? • How are they working together with other children?	• How is the child expressing their voice? • How are they showing their preferences? • What are the circumstances when they are being listened to by his/her peers?

Sub themes

Motivation	Problem Solving	Coordination	Imagination	Empathy
• How are they actively involved? • How do they maintain their play?	• How do they communicate with others to articulate their ideas? • In what ways do they show a creative response in their play?	• How are their movements reflecting their emotional state? • How are they showing capacity to adapt?	• How are they using resources imaginatively? • How are they acting out their ideas?	• How do they support other children emotionally and physically? • How do they show their feelings?

Prompts

Risk taking Challenge Persistence Initiative Interest	Determination Instruction Knowledge Negotiation Supporting role	Verbal communication Sharing Non-verbal communication Attracting attention Interest Negotiating Supporting role	Flexible environment Flexible resources Involving an adult	Following Listening

They all stop for a moment and take in what has happened. The two boys start to laugh; they pick up half of the stick and wave it around making whooshing noises. Michael has the other half which is much more manageable in length now and he copies the boys, holding it out like a sword and copying the same movement. All the boys are laughing now as they continue their pretend sword game.

Observing empowerment in play 79

FIGURE 6.3 The moment the stick breaks in two

Here is the written commentary from the educator soon after the event; it focuses on ownership and coordination.

OWNERSHIP

How is the child showing their familiarity with the play environment?
   Confident to be on his own in the field and go to the edge of the boundary. Most children stay in the middle. He wants to explore the long grass on his own.

How is he embracing play?
   Shows excitement when he finds the stick. There is a physical reaction as well as a verbal one. Sense that he wants to share his discovery by taking it over to the other boys but also that he wants to keep hold of it.

What is his vested interest in the play?
   The stick, and that he wants to keep hold of it.

What are the commonalities between the children?
   They all want the stick!

How is Michael in control of the play?
   He is making decisions as the play progresses:

1. He goes towards the boys.
2. When he realises they want the stick he runs away with it.

3. He knows it is going to be difficult to keep hold of the stick, two against one, in a pulling action, so he turns changing the direction of the stick.
4. When the stick breaks, he has the choice to feel upset or to join a new game.
5. His choice to be part of the new game shows his adaptability and that he wants to be part of play with other children.

Michael is also determined – he is not going to give the stick up easily even though it is two against one. He made the decision to take the stick towards the two boys. He could have kept it to himself at the edge of the field so that suggests he wanted to share his discovery.

How is he working together with other children?

He is not working with the other boys to start with. He wants to keep the stick as he found it in the first place. When the stick is broken in half, he then joins in the imaginary game that the others have initiated.

Coordination

How are the child's actions reflecting their emotional state?
- Defiant verbal communication – 'It's my stick! Let go!'.
- Confident – walking over with the stick in the first place, wanting to show the other boys what he has found, but perhaps not expecting their reaction to want to take it off him.
- Determined to keep hold of the stick.
- Persisting in making sure he is in control of the stick even if sometimes it looks like he is going to lose it.

How is he showing his capacity to adapt?

When the stick has snapped in two, Michael could have reacted badly, but instead he accepted the situation and played along with the new imaginary game of swords. The stick was adaptable enough to let him do this, as was the environment with no set outcomes or rules.

The educator reflected on Michael's play after reviewing the video footage:

> Michael could have easily gone to an adult to try and get his stick back when the boys were so close to taking it from him, but he showed his determination and persistence in sorting it out for himself. I think that's because there wasn't an adult immediately to hand. I'm surprised, because he usually gives up on things quite quickly if they are not going his way. There was obviously something important to him for him to want to keep the stick. I think you can see that when he finds it and gives a little squeal. He is excited, and I suppose taking it over to the other children was a way in which he could share that excitement, although I don't think he was expecting them to try and take it off him.

On the process of observing play using the empowerment framework she reflected:

> Filming Michael's play meant that I didn't have to think on my feet and try and write down everything he was doing. It all happened too quickly for that and I think that is why it is easy to dismiss play as a non-event and why people think children aren't doing anything when they play. Being able to review the video and then make my observation through the question prompts made me think deeper than the superficial 'he did this, he did that'.
>
> Doing observations in this way has meant reorganising our team a bit. I would have normally supported the structured activity that happened after outdoor play, but we agreed that I could review the video and Kate would take responsibility for the activity so it re-distributed our jobs. This meant that I could write up the observation whilst it was still fresh in my mind and I didn't have to leave it until the end of the day when I was tired and didn't want to face a load of paperwork.

The empowerment framework provides a way in which children's actions and reactions in play can be analysed at a slower pace and can be revisited. It also means that video can be shared with parents and other educators. If video is stored appropriately, it can be a valuable asset in showing children's progress at their time in a setting. Michael's parents were delighted to receive a copy of his play during his time at the nursery. It gave them an insight into what and who he played with and also enabled them to see connections between his play at home. Recognising children's experiences in play and that they support a process of empowerment can contribute to a new way for educators to plan and reflect upon pedagogic practice. Michael's setting is reviewing how staff are utilised at different points during the daily routine so video observations can be reviewed and reflected upon. A picture of empowerment for each child is then developed over time.

In the next example Amy and Jade are indoors playing with a toy boat, small figures and a railway track.

Voice and empathy: Amy's boat play

A boy is sitting on the floor of the nursery in the middle of a wooden railway track. Other children including Jade are on the opposite side of the track, trying to fix the train so it can be pushed along the track. The boy is watching as the children are having a discussion about the train as they try to figure out how it aligns onto the track. Amy comes along with a toy boat. It is quite large and she is struggling to carry it. The boy reaches out his arms as if to say that he will help her. She doesn't see him or the train track and stumbles over it, nearly dropping the boat. She is now in the middle of the track with the boy and puts the boat down next to him. She goes to the other side of the room and gets a box of small world figures and brings it over to him (see Figure 6.4). She sits down next to him and gestures to him to play with her by passing him a figure, taking one herself and

82 Observing empowerment in play

FIGURE 6.4 Small world play

putting her figure in the boat. The boy watches, and then starts to join in. They are not talking very much, but making whooshing noises like the sea and Amy makes her figure jump off the boat onto the carpet and then repeats this over and over. The boy puts his figure on the mast of the boat, trying to balance it there.

Jade comes over, having finished with the train, and watches what Amy and the boy are doing. She sits down beside them and has a look in the box of small world items. She takes out a figure, looks carefully at it and announces, 'this one has a funny face!' Amy turns towards her to take a look. She smiles. Jade moves closer and starts to include her figure with Amy's and the boy's play so that all the figures are now sharing the boat. The children are using different parts of the boat; the boy has moved his figure to the helm, whilst Jade is attaching her figure to the mast. Amy is turning a part on the deck of the boat around and around. Jade sees her doing this and wants to have a go. There is a slight disagreement about this and Jade stands up, leans over Amy with her arms outstretched to get to the toy. Amy shuffles backwards away from the play. She watches for a moment as Jade takes over the deck part of the boat. She seems unsure what to do and puts her thumb in her mouth. She mumbles something and points towards the boat with her other hand. She then moves closer to the boat, picks up a figure and positions herself opposite Jade, close to the boy who smiles at her and they continue playing.

Observing empowerment in play   83

The nature of examining children's choices and natural interactions with other children requires consideration of the meanings that emerge from their experiences and perspectives on play. Initially it might seem that there is not much happening in Amy's play and the educator reviewing the video had to watch it several times to make the following observations.

VOICE

How is the child expressing their voice?

The children are not shouting or being loud in their play. They are using their voice in more subtle ways such as eye contact, smiling at each other, a sign of encouragement that they want to play together. They are expressing what they want though their movement around the boat – the way Jade stands over Amy to try and dominate her and the way Amy chooses to still be part of the play even when it seems Jade has taken over.

How are they showing their preferences?

Amy initiates the play by carrying the boat to where the boy is sitting. Not sure if she was intending to stop there, but almost tripping over makes up her mind to stay. She chooses to get the box of small world figures and the boy is happy to play alongside her.

Jade wants to be part of the play, although initially she is probably just being a bit nosy and likes to be involved in whatever anyone else is doing. The fact that all the children stay when there is a slight disagreement over the boat shows that they make a choice to be part of the play.

Amy shows her ability to compromise – Jade shows that she has learnt how to use her physicality to get what she wants by standing over Amy, almost pushing her out.

What are the circumstances when they are being listened to by his/her peers?

They are being listened to through their responses rather than what is being said or heard. The exchange of smiles means that they want each other to play, the eye contact between them gives each of them reassurance.

Amy protests when Jade tries to muscle in on the part of the boat she is playing with, but does not take her on and Jade ignores her – not listening in the traditional sense but indicating that Jade is more in a position of control than Amy. However Amy still finds a way to be part of the play which says to me that she is more resilient.

Empathy

How do they support other children emotionally and physically?

- The boy holds out his arms as if to want to help Amy because the boat is quite large and she seems to be struggling to carry it.

- After Jade has been dominant, Amy seeks out the boy who does not reject her and he makes space for her to play next to him.
- Amy and the boy have regular eye contact and exchange smiles, encouraging them both to continue with the play.

How do they show their feelings?

- Smiling and eye contact with each other.
- Sharing the boat and small world figures.
- Amy verbally protests when Jade stands and leans over her.
- Amy shows her vulnerability when she puts her thumb in her mouth and moves backwards away from the play.
- Jade uses her physical presence to be dominant by standing up and leaning over Amy; she has done this before and knows it is a successful strategy to get her own way over other children.

It is important to view the process of empowerment holistically, that is not just observing children's actions and interactions with other children, but knowing children's preferences as well as considering the views of others closely associated with them. The approach to observing empowerment in play needs to be flexible, led by children's choices, but this can be challenging and it is a skill to record meaningful observations as the key worker for Amy explains here:

> That was so hard to observe! I didn't know what to put down at first as it looked like nothing was happening! It took me quite a while to think about it from a voice and empathy perspective rather than just reporting on what they were doing such as using their fine motor skills to move the figures.

The manager of the setting also reflected on how using the empowerment framework has worked in practice:

> It will take time to adapt to this way of thinking. As a setting we haven't focused on empowerment before. We look for the areas of learning to meet the curriculum requirements. I can see how looking for empowerment also meets learning criteria but it really means developing a new set of skills and this will take some time and effort as a team.

An important aspect of the empowerment framework is examining children's social worlds, the realities of their play and how they make and sustain connections with other children. The aim is to understand children's individual and group actions and decisions based on their interactions with other children; to build an account of children's social play in order to develop a picture of how it contributes to their process of

Observing empowerment in play 85

empowerment. Exploring social worlds of children, the cultural influences upon them, and on their actions and ideas provides a platform for understanding the wider context of children's play and empowerment. It also supports an examination of the norms and values associated with particular individuals and groups such as early childhood educators and parents. In the next example Harry and Edward, who are friends outside of the settings they attend, are at Harry's house, playing outdoors with a water butt.

Participation and problem-solving: Harry and Edward's water butt play

Harry and Edward are at Harry's house playing in the garden. They have just come back from forest school, splashing in the mud puddles there, and want to continue playing with water. The only water available to them in Harry's garden is a water butt (Figure 6.5). Harry goes over to it immediately and tries to turn on the tap located at the bottom of the butt. He struggles to get it to turn on. It appears he doesn't remember how to do it and is trying all different ways to make the water flow. Edward, who has been watching, tries to take over. He is a bit stronger than Harry and manages to turn the tap. Suddenly a spurt of water comes out and both boys squeal in delight. Harry rushes over to the vegetable patch to retrieve a watering can. He puts it under the flow of water to catch it. Edward turns off the

FIGURE 6.5 The boys at the water butt

tap to Harry's protest because his watering can has not filled up yet. Edward ignores him and goes off to find his own container. When he comes back, he finds Harry trying to turn the tap on again, but he is not strong enough. Edward pushes him out of the way and easily turns it on and fills up his container. He then takes it over to the vegetable patch and pours it into the soil. Edward has left the tap running and Harry experiments with it, turning it just a bit so it restricts the flow of water to a trickle without turning it off completely. He then turns it the other way so the flow is increased. He stands up and puts his feet under the water flow, getting his shoes wet. He laughs out loud. Happy with what he has found out he can do, he swaps with Edward and takes his watering can to a different vegetable bed and sprinkles the water over the plants from the spout. Edward watches and shouts, 'hey, I want one of those!' Harry responds, 'we only got one!' Edward goes towards Harry to take it from him, but Harry runs away laughing. The boys have forgotten the water is still running and Harry's mother shouts to him to turn the water off.

Connections can emerge between different contexts on children's lived experiences. Views of parents and observing play in informal situations can help to 'knit together threads of evidence' (Brooker, 2002, p. 84) to generate an overall picture of the child and their interests and motivations. This provides a basis for understanding traditions and shared experiences that exist within a family and can also highlight the underlying values and beliefs about play in an early childhood setting. For example, Harry and Edward had both just enjoyed playing with water at forest school. They continued their exploration of water at home, in a different context but with the same fascination. The ability to do this demonstrates how home life, setting life and shared understanding of values associated with everyday activities such as growing vegetables compound cultural norms and activities.

Harry's mother was happy for the video to be shared with the 'stay and play' educator at the forest school. She analysed the observation, focusing on participation and problem-solving.

PARTICIPATION

Where is the child positioning themselves within the play?

They both want to get to the water butt and have a go, but the space is quite restricted so they either have to fight for it or take turns. There is a bit of pushing going on to start with, but they seem to understand that they need each other – it is Harry's garden and water butt, but Edward can turn on the tap.

Harry is quite clever in leaving Edward to it when he realises he can't turn the tap on and goes to find the watering can. I suspect he has figured out that Edward will want it and Harry knows that there is only one in the garden, so by getting it first he has an advantage.

How are they negotiating with others?

Each of the boys have their strengths – Edward is stronger and outgoing, Harry is quiet but can think around situations much better. Harry knows that it is no good trying to argue with Edward as he won't win either physically or verbally because Edward just shouts louder. Harry finds other ways to negotiate, the watering can, and changing the focus away from the water butt to running around the garden at the end.

How are they taking part?

They both want to be involved in the water and making it come out of the container. After the initial tussle of trying to turn the tap on, they share the water and Harry experiments with the flow of water and getting his shoes wet. They are both involved and concentrating on the water butt. They knew exactly what they wanted to do as soon as they got into the garden.

What choices and decisions are they making to be involved in the play?

The water is important and they both want to be involved in exploring what they can do with it. Harry wants to find out how he can manage to turn the tap on and off on his own. He knows that he can't turn it completely off and on as he is not strong enough, but he is able to adapt the flow of water. This shows his ability to experiment and learn from trying out different strategies. Harry also makes the decision to move away from Edward when he knows he won't be able to use the tap whilst Edward is in control of it.

Edward uses his physicality (he is bigger and stronger than most of his peers) to get his own way. He does that here, knowing that he is stronger than Harry and has a good chance of being able to turn the tap on.

Problem-solving

How do they communicate with others to articulate their ideas?

Harry was clever in his problem solving in understanding how much strength was needed for him to turn the tap off and on. He had tried to turn it on from the off position and knew that he couldn't do it. He was testing his strength in altering the flow of the water. In getting the watering can, he was also suggesting ideas to Edward about how they could play with the water butt.

In what ways do they show a creative response in their play?

Getting his feet wet showed how Harry was testing out the water and not just using it in the intended way to collect water for the plants. He held his feet under the water for a good few seconds to feel how it soaked his foot and trainers. He also knew when he showed Edward the effect of pouring the water from the can that he would want to have a go. He made sure that he was a good distance from Edward so that when he came to take the watering can from him, he had a chance of running away from him.

Looking for the underlying connections between children, their families and early childhood settings is significant in terms of gaining an understanding of the broader social philosophy and values around the subject of children's play and its role in their development. The empowerment framework is best utilised when these issues are thought about and addressed as part of a holistic view of children's empowering experiences. The educator knew both children very well and so was able to comment on what she thought was going through their minds as they played with the water butt. Her analysis of the situation made sense to Harry's mother who commented:

> It makes sense that he was testing out how far he could turn the tap because he likes to be independent and gets frustrated when he can't do something. It is interesting to see the concentration on his face whilst he is doing it and since then, I have noticed that he has tried to turn the tap on and has had some success. He definitely brings home ideas from nursery and the 'stay and play' sessions. He is always trying to recreate what he has done there at home. I noticed yesterday that he was building a castle and when I asked what it was for, he said they had made one at nursery.

The educator also reflected:

> It is interesting for me to see children's play at home. I don't often get to do this and it proves to me that the ideas we instil in them here transfer into their home life and vice versa. Those experiences shouldn't be separate in my view. They are all part of the learning experience and that's why parent partnerships are so important so we all understand what is significant for an individual child and how we as professionals and parents can give them positive experiences.

It is important to consider the meanings children attach to their actions, and attempting to analyse the underlying intentions and decisions that appear to inform them is significant in understanding children's behaviour. It is also unavoidable to draw on personal cultural values when interpreting children's play actions and choices, but making connections with parents' and other professionals' views supports the basis for a web of perspectives. Consequently the choices made in observing play and empowerment, both conscious and unconscious, became entwined in the interpretive nature of play.

As stated throughout this book, any observation is interpretive because it is made from an individual's point of view. Two people observing the same social play actions of children can come up with two different interpretations of what is happening, and the extent to which they are empowered. This is made even more complex because of the ambiguous nature of the terms play and empowerment. The very nature of an interpretive paradigm creates a web of perspectives between the process of recording and analysing observations and the relationships which develop between settings, educators, children and parents. The multiple perspectives that emerge through trialling the empowerment framework contribute to a reflexive process of analysis; systematically questioning what is seen and heard to find patterns and themes that are significant to children and help to understand how empowering experiences can be developed through play. The challenge of this is time and investment of professional development to cultivate a new way of thinking about play and recording observations.

Summary

The examples in this chapter demonstrate the influence of educators' perspectives in the decisions on what to observe and their subjectivity in the interpretation of children's play. By drawing on different views from parents and colleagues who know the children, a layered picture is revealed, not only of the complex nature of play and empowerment, but also the significance of individual values and beliefs about the importance of play. A questioning approach will always provide a platform for exploring children's social worlds, and the empowerment framework enables a way in which educators can examine the intricacies of their play. The framework also supports a developing understanding of how children make and sustain connections with other children. The observations of play contribute to understanding how play can be empowering and why this is so important for children's learning, development and social relationships.

7

THE CHALLENGES OF CELEBRATING EMPOWERMENT IN PLAY

The term 'play' is used on a daily basis in early childhood practice, but it can encompass a spectrum of ideology, values and beliefs. Depending on these beliefs, children's experiences can be very different and the skills they develop to explore and be creative can range from life-affirming to feeling unable to contribute. The term 'empowerment' is also ambiguous and not clearly understood or articulated in early childhood in relation to children's development. The empowerment framework goes some way to addressing these issues and supports a focus on transformative experiences where the unpredictability and open-endedness of play is celebrated. Empowerment in play is not determined by the context, but is influenced by children's actions and reactions within that context. Empowerment therefore is not restricted by the environment or resources within it, but can be accessed by children through their interactions and the possibilities available through play.

The empowerment framework contributes a layered picture of empowerment that is based on a holistic view of children's play experiences. The super themes of participation, voice and ownership for children are based on their terms, determined by their choices and decisions, and negotiated between them in play. Therefore empowering experiences are generated between children as part of an overall shared experience. Considering play and empowerment as a process supports ongoing reflections about how play is valued, not just in formal contexts such as early childhood settings, but also by parents and the wider community.

At the beginning of this book, three key questions were posed and the preceding chapters unpack some of the complexities surrounding empowerment in play. Here, those three questions are asked again and answered in relation to understanding the process of empowerment based on the definition and three super-themes of participation, voice and ownership.

The challenges of celebrating empowerment 91

In what ways can child-initiated, social play empower children?

The analysis of children's play coupled with the views from educators and parents not only confirms the importance of participation, voice and ownership for children's empowerment, it establishes their interdependence. It leads to the identification of the skills, behaviours and types of environment that underpin a process of empowerment. This analysis corresponds with previous research into play, for example, Fromberg and Bergen (2015) suggest children's social play constantly evolves as they explore their interests, share ideas and use their environment and resources in imaginative ways. Child-initiated, social play may also empower children through the nature of play's unpredictability and open-endedness. Engaging in participatory processes, where the social dynamics are not predetermined or a final outcome expected, enables children to focus not only on play, but also the part they undertake in perhaps leading or influencing others. Cockburn (2005) suggest that the position of power that children may take on during play is important in understanding the nature of participation and negotiation. Children's active participation in play where they have an emotional investment in what is going on and wanting to be part of that situation is significant in children's motivation to be involved, have an opinion or voice within that situation and feel a sense of ownership in how play develops. The examples presented in this book have led to a conceptual framework of empowerment that not only confirms the importance of these various play experiences, dynamics and processes, but also offers a way of understanding how these contribute to the themes of participation, voice and ownership (see Figure 7.1).

FIGURE 7.1 The empowerment framework

92 The challenges of celebrating empowerment

The sub-themes of motivation, coordination, imagination, problem-solving and empathy support the three super-themes as well as offering a categorisation of the skills that children use in play to create or sustain their involvement. The immediacy of the dynamic of play for children means that they sometimes have to think and act quickly to maintain their position in their play; for example if in leading the play a child voices a decision that other children do not like or want to participate in, they can easily walk away, re-group or override the decision. The leader of the play has to react quickly to maintain their role and the power they have over other children through using their social understanding of the situation. This complex nature of play is revealed through the analysis of continually evolving play contexts where individuals and groups of children share and explore their interests (Fromberg and Bergen, 2015). The empowerment framework illustrates the way that the play examples in Chapters 4 and 5 approach the complex nature of play with a specific focus on children's empowerment. The unpredictability and possibilities of play contribute to the subjective nature of play research, as well as multi-dimensional aspects, such as the way that children use their play environment and how they develop peer relationships in play.

What is a valid and useful definition of children's empowerment in play?

The coding and subsequent thematic analysis of the video observations of children's play resulted in a conceptual framework that identifies three super-themes, participation, voice and ownership, as key to defining children's empowerment in play. The definition of empowerment is significant in that it does not locate itself within a particular context, instead it may be universally applied to any situation where child-initiated, social play takes place. Therefore it can be accessible and transferable across different play contexts. The definition of empowerment was presented in Chapter 3 but, as a reminder, here it is again:

PARTICIPATION

Empowerment in child-initiated, social play is not one single action, event or circumstance. It is concerned with examining individual choices and decisions based on social interactions, emotional responses and environmental influences within situated boundaries and resources. There are essential components that contribute to young children's experiences of empowerment; these are participation, voice and ownership.

The process of empowerment in child-initiated, social play is made up of interactions with other children which may influence the motivation or direction of play. How children decide to participate in play is significant. They may negotiate their way into a play situation, or be more assertive through taking the lead and instructing other children. They may challenge themselves through pushing their physical limits or encourage other children to try something new in order to sustain play. Children may use their initiative to change the game or focus of the play to ensure that it continues. Becoming involved in established social play is also an emotional risk children take in joining in for the first time or expressing their interest in case they are rejected by the group.

Voice

Empowerment in children's play also manifests itself through children expressing their point of view in agreement or opposition with others and using different modes of expression to show their preferences. This may be through making decisions about the materials or resources they want to play with, the space they want to play in or the timing of their play. Expressing an opinion amongst other children who also have opinions requires confidence and self-assurance, especially in a large social group. Through different ways of communicating with their peers, and having their opinions valued and heard by others, children are more willing to contribute their thoughts and ideas.

Ownership

Children want to feel that they are part of something, for example a family, an early childhood setting, or part of a wider community. When children have a sense of ownership they engage with and support other children through their actions and interest in what is happening around them. When children are able to engage with materials in different and creative ways, they have the opportunity to express independent thought and be able to follow it through to a conclusion of their own satisfaction. It is an emotive response of being included and a tangible experience of sharing something that has happened, been created or achieved together.

Parents' and educators' views about articulating empowerment

As well as thinking about the significance of children's empowerment, the extent to which play is embedded in the culture of early childhood settings and the wider community is an important consideration. Educators and parents reflected on the value placed on children's play and recognised that the ambiguities regarding play and empowerment presents challenges in their thinking and decision-making when providing play opportunities for children. This is because of the fluid and unpredictable nature of what happens in children's play and the need for educators to constantly evaluate and reflect upon their role in supporting play, their understanding of play and empowerment – which are already identified as ambiguous terms – and how they might challenge themselves to ensure their practice is a true reflection of their values and beliefs. When asked to explain what empowerment meant in practice, one educator suggested: 'Children's empowerment for me is when a child can walk into a room and know exactly who they might want to speak to and that they can join in and that they don't need to hold back.'

Some educators focused on the importance of children's experiences from the perspective of what it must be like for children to be involved in different play situations while others discussed how they responded to the requirement to support children to have those experiences within their settings. Many talked about how this was an intuitive part of their professional role rather than something planned:

> Empowerment is not something I am conscious of but I think it is something that I am doing, you know, helping children to be empowered because I am interested in what they are doing, want to help them learn, want to listen to their views, perhaps challenge them now and again to get them to think about what they are doing. I don't think that makes me stand out, if you know what I mean, it is just part of what I do on a daily basis. If that is supporting children's empowerment, then great.

Educators' responses also focused on the social dynamics of children's play. They were aware of the significance of children's interactions with other children and how those may encourage a process of empowerment (Jiang et al., 2011). The lead educator of the children's centre explains how she recognises that children's ability to coordinate their actions and physical presence in a play space can help them become empowered, just by being part of something:

> They are just starting to play socially and I think that is a really important moment, when they accept each other and recognise that it is more fun being together than on their own, even if initially that is a bit scary with children they don't know so well. But once they are in the play they become more confident and move the game on as a group.

The views of parents also contribute to understanding the balance required between what children *need* from their play experience and what is *expected* from play by adults. Lester and Russell (2008) are sceptical about how parents see and evaluate play, suggesting that play is only approved of when it meets planned objectives or demonstrates socially acceptable behaviour. This has not been the case in this research; the views of parents and educators have been very accepting of play as an important aspect of children's lives and have given important insight into children's play preferences. However, throughout the interviews with parents and educators there was a tendency to see play as something separate, fitted around other, more important things. This is reflected in the extract from a lead educator recalling a conversation with a parent about taking their child for a walk which is also discussed in Chapter 5. Here it is again as a reminder:

> One parent said 'we go for a walk in the fields all the time', but the other day she said, 'we didn't walk, we stopped and did what he wanted to do and that

was because of forest school, because we did forest school [at the children's centre] and I didn't realise that he wanted to do all of these things'. That was maybe investigating the insects or making a den or just standing still and looking at things, and she [the parent] said, 'that was a real eye opener for me, we used to go for this walk and I used to think I was providing this wonderful experience for him, but actually I wasn't doing what he wanted to do, I was doing what I thought he wanted to do. When we go now, we don't go as far, we don't need to go as far and we just go at his pace'. For me that is empowerment, for the child to be able to own that experience and be able to get that across to his parent.

Initially the parent thought the walk and the length of the walk was the most important thing, not what the child was engaged in whilst exploring. McInnes et al. (2011, p. 123) suggests that 'a lack of understanding of play combined with a mistrust of child-led activities and reluctance to give children choice and control, results in an over-reliance on adult led activities with adults having control and choice'. In all of the settings and home contexts there were elements of mistrust of child-initiated play, with subtle comments made to children, such as 'only for five minutes', 'I'm watching you' or 'are you sure you want to do that?', therefore establishing a sense of control, even if from a distance. These comments were made in the general conversation between children, parents and educators, and were generally 'throwaway' comments, which on their own may seem harmless, but which can accumulate, contributing to the de-valuing of the role of play. One lead educator commented:

> I know play is important, but there is so much to fit in during the week that has to be officially recorded in my setting and so play is something that the children do when we are busy writing up learning logs or planning the next activities. I have never thought that play actually gives me everything I need to complete those observations and tick those developmental boxes. I guess that's about me wanting to be in control, wanting to make sure I can cover everything, when actually just standing back and observing children's play can give me lots of those indicators. That's hard for me though. I feel I'm not doing my job if I am not 'teaching' something.

Some of the challenges for early childhood educators in wanting to encourage child-initiated play in practice may be because of a limited knowledge and understanding of play (McInnes et al., 2011), parental attitudes towards play influencing what they do in practice (Fung and Cheng, 2012), confidence in their ability to champion play and its benefits, or the demands of the curricula (Wood, 2010). Nolan and Kilderry (2010) acknowledge that educators need to be active learners in their context, rather than passive consumers of policies and newly emerging theoretical ideas. They define this as professional learning where perspectives are shared in a collegial and respectful environment. Fresh professional perspectives can be achieved when educators have a deeper understanding of their own beliefs and experiences and where they allow multiple perspectives and approaches to inform their practice (Leshem and Trafford, 2006). Consequently scrutinising research into areas such as parental attitudes towards play may support educators in developing their knowledge and understanding (Veitch et al., 2006).

The cultural and pedagogical beliefs surrounding play are significant in how play is valued in a setting or context and how those values translate into everyday opportunities for child-initiated play. In the examples in Chapters 4 and 5 educators across the different settings understood the significance and importance of children's play. They were aware of the benefits of child-initiated play for personal, social and emotional development and yet seemed to not realise the potential for children's empowerment in these play situations. Therefore, if the challenge is to enhance early childhood settings' recognition and instantiation of the potential for children's empowerment in play, one question must be how far those settings and individuals who work there have to change their thinking and practice.

How can articulating children's empowerment in play support early childhood practice?

As suggested in the previous chapter, the thinking and practice behind observing young children would need to change if empowerment in play were to become more prominent in early childhood practice. However there is some evidence that change is possible. Stephen (2010, p. 15) recognises that the 'landscape of provision is shifting' and so in considering children's experiences in different contexts empowerment is a concept that could thread through those experiences to support holistic development. Observations of practice are often interpreted in different ways and sometimes this may cause tension between thinking and practice (Sylva and Pugh, 2005). Therefore an important implication of the research into children's empowerment is that educators need to talk to each other, sharing their values and beliefs about children's play. Being actively involved in continuous professional development which focuses on active discussion about the significance of children's play as well as being self-reflective about how different play situations are interpreted supports an ongoing debate about children's empowerment in play. The sharing of values and approaches to practice may also support understanding inconsistencies in the way play is observed and interpreted.

Values about children's play and empowerment

Knowledge and understanding about play is constantly evolving and even in an early childhood setting, conflicting views can surface where approaches and values about play are openly discussed amongst educators about how to support quality play experiences. Bennett et al. (1997) argue that the type of early childhood setting experienced by children is in part determined by educators' understanding of play and therefore it is important that different values about play and where they come from are recognised. Being open to different perspectives on children's play supports a 'can do' disposition towards children which Kalliala (2009) argues relates to educators as 'activators' who can identify children's interests and support subsequent play to develop. Educators as activators need to be aware of power relationships that exist between children and adults and also the power dynamics of the setting. This awareness supports a reflective approach to understanding practitioners' values and beliefs which can then be explored in relation to the decisions they make in supporting children's play. Brown (2003, p. 58) suggests that 'children who have little control over their world inevitably have fewer positive experiences, which in turn slows the development of their self-confidence ... children who lack confidence are less likely to take risks or try out different solutions to problems they encounter'. The same can be argued to be true for educators expressing their understanding about play, as considering values and beliefs and engaging in self-reflection on personal practice is challenging (Canning, 2010; Howard, 2010). Not only is it important to recognise and analyse current working practices, but also to understand how they have evolved and on what basis they were implemented. Acknowledging these factors supports understanding of the power relationships that exist in relation to educators' ability to express their views about children's play. As a setting, the city centre private day nursery found reviewing the video footage of their children a focal point for debating underlying fundamental beliefs about play. One key worker reflected:

> Watching the video of Milo's play back enabled us to have a discussion about what we knew about him as a child and what we thought we knew about his play. What we perceived and what we actually saw on the video was very different. This made me think about what I take for granted on a daily basis and how much I take play for granted. I am going to watch more carefully, think about the factors that influence play more closely so that I can understand the children in my care better.

If discussions about play are not challenging enough, adding the dimension of children's empowerment adds a further layer of complexity. Recognising empowerment is subjective because it is also about interpreting children's actions and interactions. Those decisions about how a child is navigating a process of empowerment is based on knowledge and understanding about the relationship between play and empowerment. Therefore, it is not only debating play that is important for settings, but also recognising the balance of power dynamics and how they influence the ability for children to enter into a process of empowerment. Exploring children's empowerment adds to the debate about the significance of the context and experience of children's play, and how children make sense of the world around them (Pramling Samuelsson and Carlsson, 2008; Moyles, 2010; Rogers, 2011). In practice, making connections between children's play and empowerment may support understanding of every aspect of the child, influencing the way in which educators work with individual children. One key worker at the city centre private day nursery commented:

It's hard to define [empowerment] because it's not something I think about every day, it's not top of my list of priorities, but I just want children to have choices, be confident to make those choices and be able to change their mind if they want to.

A focus on children's experiences

The concept of empowerment through play supports a reflection of children's experiences rather than adult influences or expectations and recognises children's 'capacity for positive development, enhanced through access to the broadest range of environments and play opportunities' (Playwork Principles Scrutiny Group, 2005; Brown, 2008). Through play children are able to make their own choices and decisions and influence each other. Their play reflects what they already know and their opinions about the world which Sandberg and Vuorinen (2010) suggest is because children's thinking and actions are shaped by the intellectual, language and psychological tools used every day in their immediate environment. The cultural context of play contributes to understanding social interactions between children where connections are made through sharing and relating to each other's ideas. The three super-themes of participation, voice and ownership relate to children's experiences in their play and support a process of empowerment.

Play is a fluid interplay between experiences, imagination and curiosity which support children's development and understanding of the world. However, philosophies of play encompass a spectrum of ideology and perspectives as outlined in Chapter 2 and defining what play is and what it means can be complex and subjective dependent upon cultural influences and personal emphasis (Sutton Smith, 1997). Consequently, the discourse that most closely aligns with individual values and beliefs determines the direction of professional practice and the subsequent play opportunities children engage with. The connection between children's play and empowerment influences practice decisions in relation to valuing the process of empowerment and opportunities for child-initiated play. A childminder, who was interviewed, commented: 'Experiences are really important for empowerment; what children see, hear and who they interact with really inspires them in their play.'

Observations of child-initiated, social play experiences and consideration of these in relation to the process of empowerment provides a basis for thinking about the significance of children's empowerment in play. These interactions represent the cultural constructions and meanings associated with empowerment through play. The ethnographic nature of delving into the ideology behind play and empowerment in individual settings requires trust and openness between educators and parents. Short video recording in settings is generally accepted as part of everyday practice and parents also enjoy filming at home. Those filming opportunities hardly ever come together so that children's play experiences at home and in settings can be compared and celebrated. Sharing this type of observation can support positive and trusting relationships between parents and educators. These relationships are essential in exploring thoughts and feelings about children's play and thinking about empowerment. Participants focusing upon a common interest such as children's play nearly always feel more comfortable in offering their opinions as well as examining their own values and beliefs. This can lead to important discussions, not only about play, but about the different experiences and opportunities given to young children.

Play in settings and the home environment

Play can happen anywhere and so it is important that investigation into play is not restricted to organised learning based contexts (Hughes, 2001). In this book, the examples reflect different types of early childhood settings, children's home environments and indoor and outdoor spaces. Given the theoretical underpinning of a sociocultural approach it is important that different play environments are examined because the play experience in, for example, a childminder setting will be different to that in a private day nursery where there are more children, different resources and potentially different approaches to supporting play. From the seven case study children three of them attended multiple settings. Harry attended the city centre private day nursery and the children's centre; Jade and Michael attended the rural private day nursery and a childminder. Children adapt resources and space they have to explore and experiment with ideas, and Pramling Samuelsson and Carlsson (2008) argue that the context of children's experiences and how they make sense of what they are doing contributes to creative play experiences.

Children's play preferences are evident regardless of the environment. In their play children are adaptable; they compromise and improvise within the environment and resources available to them. A play environment can also ignite children's exploration and curiosity, allowing potential for following interests and experimenting with ideas as in the example of Michael and Tom experimenting with the tyres to climb and slide down the pole in Chapter 5. Rogers (2000) suggests that connections are made with the environment while children play, stimulating opportunities for self-expression, problem-solving, communication and building social relationships. Play contexts demonstrate that the environment, whatever and wherever that might be, enables children to experiment with ideas and use the resources available to them in new ways. Through playing children participate in shared experiences with other children and make meaningful connections that they can revisit in different play situations and contexts. The empowerment framework illustrates how the sub- and super-themes are not context-specific and the examples of children's play in this book show that children are able to follow their play interests regardless of the environment and can adapt and extend their play into different contexts.

This is particularly evident when children are observed playing in their home environment, either with peers or their siblings. They are surrounded by familiar resources and confident in their play space regardless of location within the home, for example, the garden, family space or children's bedrooms. Many of the resources in the children's home environment reflect the resources of early childhood settings:

small world toys, cars, trains and, outside, climbing frames and sandpits. The example of Milo show-jumping in Chapter 4 is an illustration of the sub-theme of imagination and in his home environment Milo demonstrates his physical skill and imagination in using outside furniture and the landscape of the garden as jumps. Pramling Samuelsson and Carlsson (2008) suggest that children find ways to symbolise and use objects that are meaningful to them when they are absorbed and confident in their environment.

Use of video review for professional development

The examples throughout the book are based on non-participant video observation to capture child-initiated, social play. The footage is non-invasive of the children's play space as the camera's zoom features minimise children's self-conscious behaviour. The results from the footage provide a fascinating insight into children's play and their interactions with other children. At the city centre, private day nursery the owner/manager of the setting asked for some staff development sessions based around the video data. With permission of the children's parents, sequences of Milo and Harry's play from home were shown to the whole staff team and resulted in stimulating discussion, not only specific to the children's play, but also to wider issues about practice, observation, assessment and planning. Howard (2010, p. 93) argues that practitioners are often susceptible to adopting a structured activity approach where learning is more easily observed as it allows them to 'manage parental pressure for academic achievement and at the same time protect their own accountability'. Through discussions with staff it emerged that although practitioners understood the benefits of play, they did not consider themselves to be play professionals although they wanted to promote a play-based curriculum.

Practitioners expressed their uncertainty about supporting children's play because they found play challenging to articulate. Brooker (2011) argues that talking about play will always start with 'it depends ...' because of the age range that play extends to, cultural and socio-economic influences and the different contexts where play occurs are unique to every situation. Consequently, developing a strong knowledge base of play as Howard (2010) suggests is more complex than it might first appear. The overriding conclusion from the staff development sessions was that most had never considered analysing play in such detail and the videos enabled sequences of play to be replayed and discussed at length. Sherin and Van Es (2005) consider video to be an insightful means of reviewing what happens in the classroom, providing space to reflect on the interactions between adults and children. The ability to review the video sequences of Milo and Harry's play provided an opportunity for their key workers and the wider staff group to discuss and reflect on the children's play and also their role in supporting that play. The lead educator for Milo and Harry commented:

> I could see Milo climbing and jumping off the indoor climbing frame and I knew it was important that he be allowed to do it, but he kept doing it,

climbing up, jumping down, climbing up, jumping down and I just couldn't take it anymore, I thought 'he's going to have an accident in a minute' and I just had to stop him. It sounds so silly now, because it was perfectly safe and he was showing me that he was competent by the fact he kept repeating it, but I just couldn't let him continue; now I feel really bad.

Another insight from the professional development sessions was that key workers associated with Milo had not realised how in social play situations he was not as confident or articulate with his peers as he was with adults. An assumption had been made that because on a one-to-one basis with an adult or in an activity where an adult was leading, Milo would lead the discussion or made significant contributions, then he needed little support in interacting with other children. Watching and analysing different video sequences with staff revealed that Milo showed his vulnerability in social group play, which had not been identified by educators before.

As a consequence of the professional development sessions the setting is going to look into using video more frequently to capture and analyse children's play and to use it as a basis for future professional development. The use of digital cameras in all of the settings and the home environments discussed in the book is prolific and so the introduction of video is not likely to be an issue. However, some criteria for video recording is needed so that footage is not a series of random events, but focused on specific areas of practice such as child-initiated, social play.

Summary

In considering the challenges of celebrating empowerment in play it is not only about placing children at the centre of the process but the way in which young children are viewed as experts in their own play. Ailwood (2011) reflects that children's play encompasses complex negotiations and social relationships which may be acknowledged but not analysed in terms of conceptualising children's play. In overlooking the significance of play for the possibilities of an empowering process for any child, adults will always have power over children's experiences (Burke, 2008). Action of power should be held by the children involved in play and not by adults supporting it. This is explored in Chapter 3 and Foucault's (1980) concept that power in an action.

The empowerment framework shows how educators can think about children's empowerment under the three super-themes of participation, voice and ownership, and how they might start to address these in their observations of children. As a whole there is a lot of information to consider and it is reasonable that real-time observation concentrates on one super- or sub-theme or even just one of the questions outlined in Chapter 6 so that an in-depth analysis of a particular aspect of play is made. Questions and reflection may also be used alongside video reviews of children's play as part of continuous professional development.

CONCLUSION

The philosophy that play is universal and intrinsically motivated contributes to the development of a layered picture of empowerment. It is not based on one single action, event or circumstance, but supports a holistic view of children's learning and development. Child-initiated, social play is rich in opportunities for empowering experiences and the super-themes of participation, voice and ownership are determined by children's choices and decisions negotiated between them in play. Therefore empowering experiences are generated between children as part of an overall shared experience. Considering play and empowerment as a process supports ongoing reflections about how play is valued, not just in formal contexts such as early childhood settings, but also by parents and the wider community.

Highlighting contemporary debates about outcome-orientated values of play (Lester and Russell, 2008) and the significance of engaging in a process of empowerment (Rappaport, 1984; Zimmerman, 1984) supports a new way of considering what children do when they engage in child-initiated, social play. Although children's play is included in everyday practice and considered important, observations of play are mainly concerned with gathering evidence of children's activity and outcomes. If children's play is viewed from an empowerment perspective, the focus shifts from attainment to the process they actively engage in. For example, the choices children make, the creativity they show, the way they participate and negotiate relationships, the way they find their voice through their actions and reactions and the way they develop a sense of control over what they are doing and why.

Children having choice in what they want to do, having access to resources they want to play with and having the time to follow their own interests is significant. Each of these factors support a process of empowerment and the framework offers a way of understanding the relationship between children's play and empowerment and what it might look like in practice. It can be used in any context and be universally applied to any situation where play takes place and so is immediately accessible and transferable.

Adults' focus on children's play where observations centre on transformative experiences and celebrate the unpredictable nature and open-endedness of play is an important aspect of analysing the process of empowerment. Play, because of its multi-faceted nature which encompasses a spectrum of ideology, values and beliefs is not determined by the context, but is influenced by children's actions and reactions within that context. Empowerment therefore is not restricted by the environment or resources within it, but can be accessed by children through their interactions and the possibilities available through play.

Child-initiated, social play is particularly rich in opportunities for empowering experiences and the empowerment framework and supporting definition provides a structure for organising observations and reflections on children's play. Beliefs and values about children's play are not always openly articulated but the framework provides a basis for re-starting the debate about the significance of children's play and how best to support children's empowerment in practice. A different approach to professional practice would mean observing and recording children's play through analysing their participation, voice and ownership. This puts demands on the educator to consider the child at the centre of the learning and development process and to observe and interpret what they are doing in specific ways. Many educators would argue that they already put children at the centre of their practice, but the difference is what is interpreted as most important in terms of learning. For example, is developing cognitive skills more important than fostering appropriate personal and emotional responses? And what are the most effective ways to approach children's learning?

Pramling Samuelsson and Carlsson (2008) propose that in order for educators to adopt new ways of working or adopt different approaches to children's learning they need to have four core skills. They suggest it is essential for educators to:

- have a good general knowledge of child development to understand children's behaviour in different social play situations;
- have an insight into children's personal background and family circumstances;
- be able to sensitively interpret children's views;
- to show respect for children's competence and experience in their play.

This book has highlighted the significance of these skills in considering children's play in different contexts and from a sociocultural approach. Considering how children are empowered through play will help bring about a shift in early childhood thinking and observations to embrace children's otherwise hidden qualities. Recognising empowerment can make a significant contribution to children's future play experiences, confidence and enthusiasm for exploration and discovery.

REFERENCES

Ailwood, J. (2003) 'Governing early childhood education through play' *Contemporary Issues in Early Childhood*, 4(3), pp. 286–299.

Ailwood, J. (2010) 'Playing with some tensions: Poststructuralism, Foucault and early childhood education' in Brooker, L. and Edwards, S. (Eds) *Engaging play*. Maidenhead: Open University Press, pp. 210–222.

Ailwood, J. (2011) 'It's about power: Researching play, pedagogy and participation in the early years of school' in Rogers, S. (Ed.) *Rethinking play and pedagogy in early childhood education: Concepts, contexts and cultures*. Oxon: Routledge, pp. 19–31.

Albon, D. (2010) 'Postmodern and poststructural perspectives on early childhood education' in Miller, L. and Pound, L. (Eds) *Theories and approaches to learning in early years*. London: Sage, pp. 38–52.

Alexander, R. (2004) 'Still no pedagogy? Principle, pragmatism and compliance in primary education' *Cambridge Journal of Education*, 34(1), pp. 7–33.

Alldred, P. (2000) 'Dilemmas in representing the voices of children' in Ribbens, J. and Edwards, R. (Eds) *Feminist dilemmas in qualitative research: Public knowledge and private lives* (2nd Edition). London: Sage Publications, pp. 147–170.

Allison, C., Baron-Cohen, S., Wheelwright, S.J., Stone, M.H. and Muncer, S.J. (2011) 'Psychometric analysis of the empathy quotient (EQ)' *Personality and Individual Differences Journal*, 51(1), pp. 829–835.

Alverson, M. (2002) *Postmodernism and social research*. Buckingham: Open University Press.

Andrews, M. (2012) *Exploring play for early childhood studies*. London: Learning Matters.

Ashcroft, L. (1987) 'Defusing "empowering": The what and the why' *Language Arts*, 64(2), pp. 142–156.

Axline, V. (1964) *Dibs: In search of self*. London: Penguin.

Bae, B. (2009) 'Children's right to participate: Challenges in every day interactions' *European Early Childhood Education Research Journal*, 17(3), pp. 391–406.

Ball, D., Gill, T. and Spiegal, B. (2008) *Managing risk in play provision: Implementation guide*. Nottingham: DCSF Publications.

Bandura, A. (1962) 'Social learning through imitation' in Jones, M.R. (Ed.) *Nebraska symposium on motivation*. Chicago: University of Chicago Press, pp. 211–274.

Bateson, P. (2005) 'The role of play in the evolution of great apes and humans' in Pellegrini, D. and Smith, P. (Eds) *The nature of play*. New York: The Guilford Press, pp. 13–24.

Bauman, Z. and May, T. (2001) *Thinking sociologically* (2nd Edition). Oxford: Blackwell Publishing.

Bekoff, M. and Byers, J. (1981) *Animal play: Evolutionary, comparative and ecological perspectives*. Cambridge: Cambridge University Press.

Bennett, N., Wood, L. and Rogers, S. (1997) *Teaching through play*. Maidenhead: Open University Press.

Bernard, R. and Ryan, G. (2010) *Analysing qualitative data: Systematic approaches*. California: Sage Publications.

Blatchford, P., Creeser, R. and Mooney, A. (1990) 'Playground games and playtime: The children's view' *Educational Research*, 32(3), pp. 163–174.

Bodrova, E. (2008) 'Make believe play versus academic skills: A Vygotskian approach to today's dilemma of early childhood education' *European Early Childhood Education Research Journal*, 16(3), pp. 357–371.

Bonnel, P. and Lindon, J. (2000) *Playwork: A guide to good practice*. Cheltenham: Stanley Thornes Publishers.

British Educational Research Association (BERA) (2003) *Early years special interest group: Early years research pedagogy, curriculum and adult roles: Training and professionalism*. Southwell: BERA.

Brooker, L. (2002) *Starting school: Young children learning cultures*. Buckingham: Open University Press.

Brooker, L. (2011) 'Taking play seriously' in Rogers, S. (Ed.) *Rethinking play and pedagogy in early childhood education: Concepts, contexts and cultures*. Oxon: Routledge, pp. 152–164.

Brown, F. (2003) 'Compound flexibility: The role of playwork in child development' in Brown, F. (Ed.) *Playwork: Theory and practice*. Buckingham: Open University Press, pp. 51–65.

Brown, F. (2008) 'The fundamentals of playwork' in Brown, F. and Taylor, C. (Eds) *Foundations of playwork*. Maidenhead: Open University Press and McGraw-Hill, pp. 7–13.

Bruce, T. (1991) *Time to play in early childhood*. London: Hodder Stoughton.

Bruce, T. (2011) *Learning through play: For babies, toddlers and young children* (2nd Edition). Oxon: Hodder Education.

Brunson, D. and Vogt, J. (1996) 'Empowering our students and ourselves: A liberal democratic approach to the communication classroom' *Communication Education*, 45(1), pp. 73–83.

Buckley, B. (2003) *Children's communication skills: From birth to 5 years*. London: Psychology Press.

Burke, C. (2008) 'Play in focus: Children's visual voice in participative research' in Thomson, P. (Ed.) *Doing visual research with children and young people*. Oxon: Routledge, pp. 23–36.

Canning, N. (2010) 'Playing with heutagogy: Exploring strategies to empower mature learners in higher education' *Journal of Further and Higher Education*, 34(1), pp. 57–69.

Canning, N. (2011) 'Celebrating children's play choices' in Canning, N. (Ed.) *Play and practice in the early years foundation stage*. London: Sage Publications, pp. 20–33.

Canning, N. (2012) 'Exploring the concept of quality play' in Reed, M. and Canning, N. (Eds) *Implementing quality improvement and change in the early years*. London: Sage Publications, pp. 75–91.

Christensen, P. (2004) 'Children's participation in ethnographic research: Issues of power and representation' *Children and Society*, 18(2), pp. 165–176.

Clark, A. and Moss, P. (2011) *Listening to young children: The mosaic approach* (2nd Edition). London: National Children's Bureau and Joseph Rowntree Trust.

Cockburn, T. (2005) 'Children's participation in social policy: Inclusion, chimera or authenticity?' *Social Policy and Society*, 4(2), pp. 109–119.
Cohen, L., Manion, L. and Morrison, K. (2007) *Research methods in education* (6th Edition). Oxon: Routledge.
Corsaro, W.A. (2005) *The sociology of childhood* (2nd Edition). California: Pine Forge Press.
Csikszentmihalyi, M. (1997) *Creativity: Flow and the psychology of discovery and invention*. New York: Harper Perennial.
Davey, C. and Lundy, L. (2011) 'Towards greater recognition of the right to play: An analysis of Article 31 of the UNCRC' *Children and Society*, 25(1), pp. 3–14.
Deleuze, G. (1993) 'What children say' in Smith, D.W. and Greco, M.A. (Eds) *Gilles Deleuze: Essays critical and clinical*. Minneapolis: University of Minnesota Press, pp. 61–67.
Department for Children, Schools and Families (DCSF) (2009) *Learning, playing and interacting: Good practice in the early years foundation stage*. Nottingham: DCSF.
Department for Education (DfE) (2014) *Statutory framework for the early years foundation stage: Setting the standards for learning, development and care for children from birth to five*. London: Crown Copyright.
Dicks, B., Flewitt, R., Lancaster, L. and Pahl, K. (2011) 'Multimodality and ethnography: Working at the intersection' *Qualitative Research*, 11(3), pp. 227–237.
Duncan, R. and Tarulli, D. (2003) 'Play as the leading activity of the preschool period: Insights from Vygotsky, Leont'ev and Bakhtin' *Early Years Education and Development*, 14(3), pp. 271–292.
Else, P. (2014) *Making sense of play: Supporting children in their play*. Oxon: Open University Press.
Ernst, J. (2014) 'Early childhood educators' use of natural outdoor settings as learning environments: An exploratory study of beliefs, practices, and barriers' *Environmental Education Research*, 20(6), pp. 735–752.
Flewitt, R. (2006) 'Using video to investigate preschool classroom interaction: Education research assumptions and methodological practices' *Visual Communication*, 5(1), pp. 25–50.
Forman, G. (1999) 'Instant video revisiting: The video camera as a "tool of the mind" for young children', *Early Childhood Research & Practice*, 1(2), pp. 1–5.
Foucault, M. (1972) *The archaeology of knowledge*. London: Tavistock Publications.
Foucault, M. (1980) 'Truth and power' in Gordon, C. (Ed.) *Power/knowledge: Selected interviews and other writings 1972–1977, Michael Foucault*. Brighton: The Harvester Press, pp. 109–133.
Fromberg, D.P. and Bergen, D. (2015) 'Introduction' in Fromberg, D.P. and Bergen, D. (Eds) *Play from birth to twelve: Contexts, perspectives, and meanings* (3rd Edition). Oxon: Routledge, pp. 1–8.
Fung, C.K. and Cheng, D.P.W. (2012) 'Consensus or dissensus? Stakeholders' views on the role of play in learning' *Early Years*, 32(1), pp. 17–34.
Garvey, C. (1991) *Play* (2nd Edition). London: Fontana Publications.
Gill, T. (2007) *No fear: Growing up in a risk averse society*. London: Calouste Gulbenkian.
Gomm, R. (1993) 'Issues of power in health and welfare' in Walmsley, J., Reynolds, J., Shakespeare, P. and Wollef, R. (Eds) *Health, welfare and practice: Reflecting on roles and relationships*. California: Sage Publications, pp. 132–138.
Gore, J. (1993) *The struggle for pedagogies: Critical and feminist discourses as regimes of truth*. Oxon: Routledge.
Greene, S. and Hill, M. (2005) 'Researching children's experience: Methods and methodological issues' in Greene, S. and Hogan, D. (Eds) *Researching children's experiences: Approaches and methods*. London: Sage Publications, pp. 1–21.

Guilbaud, S. (2003) 'The essence of play' in Brown, F. (Ed.) *Playwork: Theory and practice*. Buckingham: Open University Press, pp. 9–17.

Hart, R. (1997) *Children's participation: The theory and practice of involving young citizens in community development and environmental care*. New York: Unicef.

Howard, J. (2002) 'Eliciting young children's perceptions of play, work and learning using the activity appreciation story procedure' *Early Child Development and Care*, 172(5), pp. 489–502.

Howard, J. (2010) 'Early years practitioners' perceptions of play: An exploration of theoretical understanding, planning and involvement, confidence and barriers to practice' *Educational and Child Psychology*, 27(4), pp. 91–102.

Howard, J. and McInnes, K. (2010) 'Thinking through the challenge of a play-based curriculum' in Moyles, J. (Ed.) *Thinking about play: Developing a reflective approach*. London: McGraw-Hill, pp. 30–44.

Hoyle, E. (1999) 'Micropolitics of educational organisations', in Strain, M., Dennison, B., Ouston, J. and Hall, V. (Eds) *Policy, leadership and professional knowledge in education*. London: Paul Chapman, pp. 42–51.

Hughes, B. (1996) *Play environments: A question of quality*. London: Playlink.

Hughes, B. (2001) *Evolutionary playwork and reflective analytical practice*. Oxon: Routledge.

Hughes, B. (2006) *Play types: Speculations and possibilities*. London: Centre for Playwork Education and Training.

Huizinga, J. (1955) *Homo Luden: A study of the play element in culture*. Boston: Beacon.

Ilardo, J. (1992) *Risk taking for personal growth*. Oakland: Harbinger Publications.

James, A. and James, A. (2004) *Constructing childhood: Theory, policy and social practice*. New York: Palgrave.

James, A., Jenks, C. and Prout, A. (1998) *Theorising childhood*. Cambridge: Polity Press.

Jeffrey, B. and Craft, A. (2006) 'Creative learning and possibility thinking' in Jeffrey, B. (Ed.) *Creative learning practices: European experiences*. London: The Tufnell Press, pp. 73–91.

Jiang, J., Sun, L. and Law, K. (2011) 'Job satisfaction and organisation structure as moderators of the effects of empowerment on organisational citizenship behaviour: A self-consistency and social exchange perspective' *International Journal of Management*, 28(3), pp. 675–693.

Kalliala, M. (2009) 'Look at me! Does the adult see the child in a Finnish day care centre?' Conference paper presented at the 19th European Early Childhood Education Research Association – Diversities in Early Childhood Education, Strasbourg, 26–29 August 2009.

Katz, L. (1998) 'What can we learn from Reggio Emilia?' in Edwards, C., Gandini, L. and Forman, G. (Eds) *The hundred languages of children: The Reggio Emilia approach to early childhood education* (2nd Edition). New Jersey: Norwood, pp. 19–40.

Kress, G. (2009) *Multimodality: A social semiotic approach to contemporary communication*. Oxon: Routledge.

Langston, A. and Abbott, L. (2005) 'Quality matters' in Abbott, L. and Langston, A. (Eds) *Birth to three matters: Supporting the framework of effective practice*. Maidenhead: Open University Press, pp. 68–78.

Layard, R., Clark, A.E., Cornaglia, F., Powdthavee, N. and Vernoit, J. (2014) 'What predicts a successful life? A life course model of well-being' *The Economic Journal*, 124(580), pp. 720–738.

Leshem, S. and Trafford, V. (2006) 'Stories as mirrors: Reflective practice in teaching and learning' *Reflective Practice*, 7(1), pp. 9–27.

Lester, S. and Russell, W. (2008) *Play for a change: Play, policy and practice: A review contemporary perspectives*. London: Play England.

Loizou, E. (2005) 'Infant humour: The theory of the absurd and the empowerment theory' *International Journal of Early Years Education*, 13(1), pp. 43–53.

Loveless, A. (2009) 'Thinking about creativity: Developing ideas, making things happen' in Wilson, A. (Ed.) *Creativity in primary education* (2nd Edition). Exeter: Learning Matters, pp. 22–35.

MacNaughton, G. (2005) *Doing Foucault in early childhood studies: Applying post-structural ideas.* Oxon: Routledge.

Malaguzzi, L. (1998) 'History, ideas and basic philosophy' in Edwards, C., Gandini, L. and Forman, G. (Eds) *The hundred languages of children: The Reggio Emilia approach to early childhood education* (2nd Edition). New Jersey: Norwood, pp. 41–90.

Martin, P. and Caro, T. (1985) 'On the function of play and its role in behavioural development' in Rosenblatt, J., Beer, C., Bushnel, M. and Slater, P. (Eds) *Advances in the study of behaviour.* New York: Academic Press, pp. 59–103.

Mason, J. (2002) *Qualitative researching* (2nd Edition). London: Sage Publications.

Mason, J. and Bolzan, N. (2010) 'Questioning understandings of children's participation: Applying a cross cultural lens' in Percy Smith, B. and Thomas, N. (Eds) *A handbook of children and young people's participation: Perspectives from theory and practice.* Oxon: Routledge, pp. 125–132.

Matthews, H. (2003) 'Children and regeneration: Setting an agenda for community participation and integration' *Children and Society*, 17(4), pp. 264–276.

Mayall, B. (2002) *Towards a sociology of childhood: Thinking from children's lives.* Maidenhead: Open University Press.

McCarry, M. (2012) 'Who benefits? A critical reflection of children and young people's participation in sensitive research' *International Journal of Social Research Methodology*, 15(1), pp. 55–68.

McInnes, K., Howard, J., Miles, G. and Crowley, K. (2011) 'Differences in practitioners' understanding of play and how this influences pedagogy and children's perceptions of play' *Early Years*, 31(2), pp. 121–133.

Mishler, E. (1986) *Research interviewing: Context and narrative.* Cambridge, MA: Harvard University Press.

Moyles, J. (1989) *Just playing?* Buckingham: Open University Press.

Moyles, J. (2005) 'Introduction' in Moyles, J. (Ed.) *The excellence of play* (2nd Edition). Maidenhead: Open University Press, pp. 1–16.

Moyles, J. (2010) 'Practitioner reflection on play and playful pedagogies' in Moyles, J. (Ed.) *Thinking about play: Developing a reflective approach.* Maidenhead: McGraw-Hill and Open University Press, pp. 13–29.

Moyles, J., Adams, S. and Musgrove, A. (2002) *SPEEL study of pedagogical effectiveness research report 363.* London: Department for Education and Skills.

Neihart, M. (1999) 'Systematic risk taking' *Roeper Review*, 21(4), pp. 289–292.

New Zealand Ministry of Education (1996) *Te Whariki: Early childhood curriculum.* Wellington: New Zealand Learning Media.

Nolan, A. and Kilderry, A (2010) 'Postdevelopmentalism and professional learning: Implications for understanding the relationship between play and pedagogy' in Brooker, L. and Edwards, S. (Eds) *Engaging play.* Maidenhead: Open University Press, pp. 108–121.

Nugin, K., Veisson, M., Tuul, M., Õun, T. and Suur, S. (2016) 'Children's reflections on play' *Playwork Practice*, 3(1), pp. 23–33.

Olsson, L.M. (2009) *Movement and experimentation in young children's learning: Deleuze and Guattari in early childhood education.* London: Routledge.

Opie, I. and Opie, P. (1969) *Children's games in street and playground.* Oxford: Oxford University Press.

O'Reilly, K. (2009) *Key concepts in ethnography.* London: Sage Publications.

Page, N. and Czuba, E. (1999) 'Empowerment: What is it?' *Journal of Extension*, 37(5), pp. 7–18.

Pellegrini, A. and Smith, P. (Eds) (2005) *The nature of play: Great apes and humans.* New York: Guilford Press.

Percy Smith, B. (2006) 'From consultation to social learning in community participation with young people' *Children, Youth and Environments,* 16(2), pp. 153–179.

Piaget, J. (1951) *Play, dreams and imitation in childhood.* Oxon: Routledge and Kegan Paul.

Playwork Principles Scrutiny Group (2005) *The playwork principles.* Cardiff: Playwork Principles Scrutiny Group.

Powell, S. (2009) 'The value of play: Constructions of play in government policy in England' *Children and Society,* 23(1), pp. 29–42.

Pramling Samuelsson, I. and Carlsson, M. (2008) 'The playing learning child: Towards a pedagogy of early childhood' *Scandinavian Journal of Educational Research,* 52(6), pp. 623–641.

Pramling Samuelsson, I. and Fleer, M. (2008) 'Commonalities and distinctions across countries' in Pramling Samuelsson, I. and Fleer, M. (Eds) *Play and learning in early childhood settings: International perspectives.* New York: Springer Verlag, pp. 173–190.

Pramling Samuelsson, I. and Johansson, E. (2006) 'Play and learning: Inseparable dimensions in preschool learning' *Early Child Development and Care,* 176(1), pp. 47–65.

Prout, A. and James, A. (1997) 'A new paradigm for the sociology of childhood? Provenance, promise and problems' in Prout, A. and James, A. (Eds) *Constructing and reconstructing childhood: Contemporary issues in the sociological study of childhood.* London: Falmer Press, pp. 7–32.

Rabinow, P. (1984) 'Introduction' in Rabinow, P. (Ed.) *The Foucault reader: An introduction to Foucault's thought.* Harmondsworth: Penguin, pp. 3–30.

Rappaport, J. (1984) 'Studies in empowerment: Introduction to the issue' *Prevention in Human Services,* 3, pp. 1–7.

Readdick, C.A. and Park, J.J. (1998) 'Achieving great heights: The climbing child' *Young Children,* 53(6), pp. 14–19.

Rivera, H. and Tharp, R. (2006) 'A native American community's involvement and empowerment to guide their children's development in the school setting' *Journal of Community Psychology,* 34(4), pp. 435–451.

Robinson, K. and Jones Diaz, C. (2006) *Diversity and difference in early childhood education.* Maidenhead: Open University Press.

Robson, S. (2010) 'Self-regulation and metacognition in young children's self-initiated play and reflective dialogue' *International Journal of Early Years Education,* 18(3), pp. 227–241.

Rogers, N. (2000) *The creative connection: Expressive arts as healing.* Ross on Wye: PCCS Books.

Rogers, S. (2011) 'Play and pedagogy: A conflict of interests?' in Rogers, S. (Ed.) *Rethinking play and pedagogy in early childhood education.* Oxon: Routledge, pp. 5–18.

Rogoff, B. (2003) *The cultural nature of human development.* Oxford: Open University Press.

Sandberg, A. and Vuorinen, T. (2010) 'Reflecting the child: Play memories and images of the child' in Brooker, L. and Edwards, S. (Eds) *Engaging play.* Maidenhead: Open University Press, pp. 54–66.

Sandseter, E. (2009) 'Characteristics of risky play' *Journal of Adventure Education and Outdoor Learning,* 9(1), pp. 3–21.

Sawyer, K. (1997) *Pretend play as improvisation: Conversation in the preschool classroom.* Washington: Lawrence Erlbaum Associates.

Sherin, M. and Van Es, E. (2005) 'Using video to support teachers' ability to notice classroom interactions' *Journal of Technology and Teacher Education,* 13(3), pp. 475–491.

Shier, H. (2001) 'Pathways to participation: Openings, opportunities and obligations' *Children and Society,* 10(4), pp. 107–117.

Silverman, D. (2001) *Interpreting qualitative data: Methods for analysing talk, text and interaction*. London: Sage Publications.

Simons, H. (1996) 'The paradox of case study' *Cambridge Journal of Education*, 26(2), pp. 225–241.

Sinclair, R. (2004) 'Participation in practice: Making it meaningful, effective and sustainable' *Children and Society*, 18(3), pp. 106–118.

Sinclair, R. and Franklin, A. (2000) *A quality protects research briefing: Young people's participation*. London: Department of Health, Research in Practice and Making Research Count.

Smith, P. (2005) 'Play: Types and functions in human development' in Ellis, B.J. and Bjorklund, D.F. (Eds) *Origins of the social mind: Evolutionary psychology and child development*. New York: Guilford Press, pp. 271–291.

Smith, P. (2010) *Children and play*. West Sussex: Wiley Blackwell.

Stephen, C. (2010) 'Pedagogy: The silent partner in early years learning' *Early Years*, 30(1), pp. 15–28.

Sutton Smith, B. (1997) *The ambiguity of play*. Cambridge, MA: Harvard University Press.

Sylva, K. and Pugh, G. (2005) 'Transforming the early years in education' *Oxford Review of Education*, 31(1), pp. 11–27.

Taguchi, H. (2010) *Going beyond the theory practice divide in early childhood education: Introducing an intra-active pedagogy*. Oxon: Routledge.

Thomas, N. (2007) 'Towards a theory of children's participation' *International Journal of Children's Rights*, 15(2), pp. 199–218.

To, S. (2009) 'Conceptualising empowerment in youth work: A qualitative analysis of Hong Kong school social workers' experiences in generating empowering practices' *International Journal of Adolescence and Youth*, 15(1), pp. 257–276.

Treseder, P. (1997) *Empowering children and young people: Training manual*. London: Save the Children and Children's Rights Office.

United Nations (1989) *United Nations Convention on the Rights of the Child* (UNCRC). Europe: UN Rights Committee.

Van Oers, B. (2010) 'Children's enculturation through play' in Brooker, L. and Edwards, S. (Eds) *Engaging play*. Maidenhead: Open University Press, pp. 195–209.

Veitch, J., Bagley, S., Ball, K. and Salmon, J. (2006) 'Where do children usually play? A qualitative study of parents' perceptions of influences on children's active free play' *Health and Place Journal*, 12(4), pp. 383–393.

Vygotsky, L. (1966) 'Play and its role in the mental development of the child' available online at www.marxists.org/archive/vygotsky/works/1933/play.htm (accessed 1 July 2019) .

Vygotsky, L. (1978) *Mind in society: The development of higher psychological processes*. Cambridge, MA: Harvard University Press.

Waller, T. (2005) 'Modern childhood: Contemporary theories and children's lives' in Waller, T. and Davis, G. (Ed.) *An introduction to early childhood: A multidisciplinary approach*. London: Paul Chapman and Sage Publications, pp. 27–46.

Waller, T. (2006) '"Be careful—don't come too close to my Octopus Tree": Recording and evaluating young children's perspectives of outdoor learning' *Children Youth and Environments*, 16(2), pp. 75–104.

Waller, T. (2014) 'Modern childhoods: Contemporary theories and children's lives' in Waller, T. and Davis, G. (Eds) *An introduction to early childhood* (3rd Edition). London: Sage Publications, pp. 27–46.

Watkins, C. and Mortimer, P. (1999) 'Pedagogy: What do we know?' in Mortimer, P. (Ed.) *Understanding pedagogy and its impact on learning*. London: Paul Chapman, pp. 20–45.

Whalen, M. (1995) 'Working toward play: Complexity in children's fantasy activities' *Language in Society*, 24(3), pp. 315–348.

Wood, E. (2010) 'Reconceptualizing the play-pedagogy relationship: From control to complexity' in Brooker, L. and Edwards, S. (Eds) *Engaging play*. Maidenhead: Open University Press, pp. 11–24.

Wright, H. (1960) 'Observational child study' in Mussen, P.H. (Ed.) *Handbook of research methods in childhood development*. London: John Wiley and Sons, pp. 71–139.

Yin, R. (2012) *Applications of case study research*. London: Sage Publications.

Zimmerman, M. (1984) 'Taking aim on empowerment research: On the distinction between individual and psychological conceptions' *American Journal of Community Psychology*, 18(1), pp. 169–177.

INDEX

Page numbers in *italics* denote figures, those in **bold** denote tables.

Abbott, L. 51
adult—child power dynamics 31–35
affect of power 30
age of case study children 7
Ailwood, J. 20, 21, 31, 101
Albon, D. 31
Allison, C. 48–49
Amy 12, *16*; motivation to play 25–26, 47; voice and empathy 81–85
Andrews, M. 46–47
Ashcroft, L. 27, 36
autonomy 19, 23, 24
Axline, V. 19

Ball, D. 40, 56
Bandura, A. 36
Bateson, P. 19
Bauman, Z. 36
beliefs 29, 39, 89, 90, 97, 98, 103
belonging 63
Bennett, N. 96–97
Bergen, D. 7, 91, 92
Blatchford, P. 21
Bodrova, E. 57
body language 46
Bonnel, P. 27
boundaries, testing of 22, 31, 32, 33, 35, 40, 56, 57
British Educational Research Association (BERA) 38
Brooker, L. 86, 100

Brown, F. 97
Buckley, B. 40

Carlsson, M. 40, 41, 99, 100, 103
challenge 46, **47**, **56**, *61*, 92
changing practices 36
child—child power dynamics 36–37
child-initiated play 2–3, 18, 19, 23–24, 39, 91–92, 96, 102, 103
childminder setting 10–11, 15
choice(s) 23, 24, 30–31, 36–37, 44–50, 63, 102
city centre children's centre setting 8–9, 15
city centre private day nursery setting 7–8, 15
Cockburn, T. 91
cognitive development 19, 22
communication 26, 41, 93, 99; non-verbal **53**; verbal 46, 49–50, **53**, **56**, **59**, **65**, 66, **68**; *see also* body language
community empowerment 35–36
confidence 22, 27, 57, 93, 97
coordination 4, 60, 61, 66, 70, **72**, 74, 92; Jade case study 51–54; Michael case study 77–81; prompt questions *76*, **78**, 80
Corsaro, W.A. 30
Craft, A. 40–41
creative play 28, 40, 41
creativity 37, 40–41, 54, 57, 102
Csikszentmialyi, M. 40
culture/cultural influences 29–30, 39, 63, 85, 98

curiosity 22, 54, 98
curriculum 37–38
Czuba, E. 27, 36

Davey, C. 24
decision-making 26, 44–50, 63, 66, 67
Deleuze, G. 30
determination 44, *61*, **65**, 66
developmental discourse of play 20, 22
diary, research 15, 17
disciplinary power 32
discourses of play 20–22
Duncan, R. 22

early childhood educators: as activators 97; essential skills for 103; interviews with 3, 14, 15; professional development 96, 100–101; views about articulating empowerment 93–96
Early Years Foundation Stage (EYFS) 37
educators *see* early childhood educators
Edward 11, 51, 71; participation in den making 64–66; participation and problem-solving 85–88
emotional cues 19
emotional development 22
emotional risk taking 40, 42, 93
emotional well-being 37
emotions 20, 21, 71
empathy 4, 60, *61*, 70, 92; Amy case study 81–85; Lucy case study 48–50; prompt questions 76, **78**, 83–84
empowerment: community 35–36; definition of 3, 26–27, 41–42, 92–93; as enabling process 27; factors contributing to 39–41, 43; holistic view of 84; nature of 26–28
empowerment framework 60–61, *61*, 76, 90, *91*, 102–103; prompt questions to guide observations 75, 76, 77, **78**, 79–80, 83–84, 86–88; as tool for observing play 75–89
environment 19, 41, 50–54, 61, 99–100, 103; as support for imagination 54–57
experience of play 97, 98–99
exploratory play 56

following 48, **50**, *61*, **68**, 70
Foucault, M. 20, 30, 31–32, 37, 101
Franklin, A. 26
freedom 24
freedom of expression 24–25
friendship 31, 36
Froebel, F. 18, 20
Fromberg, D.P. 7, 91, 92
function of play 19

Garvey, C. 21, 22
Gill, T. 40
Gore, J. 31
government 31
government policies 37
governmentality 32
Greene, S. 24
Guibaud, S.

Hall, G.S. 19
Harry 11, *16*, 100; participation and problem-solving 85–88; and power dynamics 32–35, 42; and voice in play 67–70
'have a go' attitude 46
health factors 37
Hill, M. 24
historical traditions 39
home environment 99–100
Howard, J. 19, 21–22, 32, 38, 100
Hughes, B. 19, 21, 22, 23, 24, 35, 38, 46, 53–54, 56
human factors 39–40, 41, 43

imagination 4, 22, 28, 60, 61, 70, 92, 98, 100; environment and resources as support for 54–57; Milo case study 54–57; prompt questions 76, **78**
inclusion 24, 63, 93
indicators of empowering play behaviour 44–61, 77
initiative 46, **47**, 51, *61*, **72**, 92–93
instruction 59, 60, *61*, **65**, 66
interactions between children 57–60, 61, 67, 75, 84–85, 94
interest 46, **47**, **53**, **65**, **68**, 69–70
interpretation of play 3, 18, 28, 88; subjective nature of 18–19, 22, 89
interviews 14–15; early childhood educators 3, 14, 15; parent 3, 14, 15; power relationships in 14–15
intrinsic motivation 19, 22–24, 25–26, 28, 37, 46, 53–54, 103
inventiveness 54
Isaacs, S. 18

Jade 11; coordinated play 51–54
James, Adrian L. 27
James, Allison 3, 27
Jeffrey, B. 40–41
Jiang, J. 35
Johansson, E. 67
Jones Diaz, C. 57

Kalliala, M. 97
Katz, L. 36

Kilderry, A. 95
knowledge 49, 50, 59, *61*, **65**, 71; and power 32

Langston, A. 51
learning 37; outcome-based 38; play and 18, 38; social construction of 38
Lester, S. 94
Lindon, J. 27
listening 48, **50**, *61*, 67, **68**, 70; to children 23–24
locomotor play 56
Loizou, E. 31, 32
Loveless, A. 59
Lucy 11, *16*; empathetic play 48–50
Lundy, L. 24

MacNaughton, G. 32
Maori culture 39
mastery play 56
material factors 39, 40–41, 43
May, T. 36
Mayall, B. 39
McCarry, M. 66
McInnes, K. 19, 38, 95
McMillan, M. 18
meaning making 23
memory 71
mental health 37
Michael 11, *16*, 61; ownership 70, 72–74; ownership and coordination 77–81; problem-solving 58–60
Milo 11, 100–101; imaginative play 54–57; motivating play 45–48
motivation to play 4, 22, 60, *61*, 66, 74, 92; Amy case study 25–26, 47; intrinsic 19, 22–24, 25–26, 28, 37, 46, 53–54, 102; Milo case study 45–48; prompt questions 76, **78**
Moyles, J. 19, 23, 38, 66
multimodal research approach 12–17

negotiation 26, 59, 60, 63, **65**, 66, **68**, **72**, 91, 92, 102
Neihart, M. 40
New Zealand 39
Nolan, A. 95
non-participant observations 12–13
norms 30, 85, 86
nostalgic discourse of play 20–21

observations 75–89, 103; interpretive nature of 22, 88, 89; non-participant 12–13; organisation of 14; prompt questions 75, 76, 77, **78**, 79–80, 83–84, 86–87
Olsson, L.M. 30

Opie, I. and Opie, O. 21
opinions, expression of *see* voice
O'Reilly, K. 13
outcome-based learning 38
outdoor play 51
ownership 4, 19, 26, 28, 42, 51, 58, 60, 61, 70, 71–74, 90, 91, 98, 102; of emotion or memory 71; Michael case study 70, 72–74, 77–81 prompt questions 76, **78**, 79–80; and UNCRC 24

Page, N. 27, 36
parent interviews 3, 14, 15
parent views about articulating empowerment 93–96
Park, J.J. 46
participation 4, 19, 27, 28, 41–42, 51, 60, 61, 62–66, 90, 91, 92–93, 98, 102; active 61, 63; Edward case study 64–66; Harry and Edward case study 85–88; prompt questions 76, **78**, 86–87; and UNCRC 24; and voice 67
pedagogy 37–39
persistence 44, 46, **47**, *61*
Pestalozzi, J.H. 20
physical development 22
physical health 37
Piaget, J. 18, 19
play: definitions of 19; discourses of 20–22; function of 19; regulation of 18; right to 24–25, 26, 28
play characteristic discourse 20, 21–22
play 'history' 23
playwork 19, 23
Playwork Principles Scrutiny Group 19, 23, 98
Powell, S. 25
power 27, 30, 91, 101; as action 36, 37, 101; affect of 30; disciplinary 32; fluidity of 31–32, 42–43; and knowledge 32
power relationships and dynamics, interviewer and interviewee 14–15
power relationships and dynamics in play 4, 29, 30–37; adult—child 31–35, 97; child —child 36–37; testing boundaries of 31, 32–35
Pramling Samuelsson, I. 40, 41, 67, 99, 100, 103
preferences, expression of 15, 18, 19, 35, 40, 42, 47, 63, 66, 83, 93
problem-solving 4, 23, 41, 61, 66, **72**, 74, 82, 99; Harry and Edward case study 85–88; Michael case study 58–60; prompt questions 76, **78**, 87
professional development 96; use of video review for 100–101

Rabinow, P. 20, 31, 32
Rappaport, J. 27
Readdick, C.A. 46
reality, suspension of 57
reflective diary 15, 17
reflective practice 29, 38, 97
Reggio Emilia 38, 39
regimes of truth 20, 31
regulation of play 18
research approach 3–4; multimodal 12–17
research settings 6, 7–11
resources 50–54, 61, 99, 103; as support for imagination 54–57
right to play 24–25, 26, 28
risk-taking 37, 40, 46, 51, 56, *61*, 97; emotional 40, 42, 93
Robinson, K. 57
Rogers, N. 41, 99
Rogoff, B. 30
romantic discourse of play 20–21
rough and tumble play 56
Rousseau, J.-J. 20
rules 31, 32, 33, 49, 57, 60
rural private day nursery setting 9–10, 15
Russell, W. 94

Sandberg, A. 98
Sawyer, K. 41, 54
self-efficacy 26, 36
self-esteem 26
self-expression 24–25, 41, 93, 99; *see also* voice
sharing 40, 42, *61*, **65**, 76, 93
Sherin, M. 100
Shier, H. 67, 69
Sinclair, R. 26, 63, 71
social construction of learning 38
social development 22
social relationships 24, 31, 36, 41, 57, 67, 99

sociocultural perspective 29–30
Spencer, H. 19
Steiner, R. 18
Stephen, C. 38, 96
structured activity 19
Sutton Smith, B. 18, 23
symbolic play 57

Taguchi, H. 39
talking with children 17
Tarulli, D. 22
Te Whariki 39
Thomas, N. 63
time sampling 13–14
To, S. 35
Treseder, P. 35, 63, 71, 74
truth(s) 4, 31; regimes of 20, 31

United Nations Convention on the Rights of the Child (UNCRC) 24–25

values 20, 29, 39, 85, 86, 87, 88, 89, 90, 96–97, 98, 103
Van Es, E. 100
Van Oers, B. 20, 39
verbal communication 46, 49–50, **53**, **56**, **59**, **65**, 66, **68**
video recordings 3, 12–13, 14; professional development and review of 100–101
voice 4, 27, 42, 51, 60, 61, 66–70, 90, 91, 93, 98, 102; Amy case study 81–85; Harry case study 67–70; and participation 67; prompt questions 76, **78**, 83; and UNCRC 24–25
Vuorinen, T. 98
Vygotsky, L. 22, 29, 56–57

Waller, T. 34, 51
Whalen, M. 54, 71
Wood, E. 18, 37